THE RESURRECTION OF THE CRAZED

PAUL WAINWRIGHT

Published by Earth Island Books
Pickforde Lodge
Pickforde Lane
Ticehurst
East Sussex
TN5 7BN

www.earthislandbooks.com

ISBN 9781916864061

Printed and bound by Solopress, Southend

This book is dedicated to Dawn, Holly and my Mum.

In memory of my Dad, Ronald, who is forever missed.

Many thanks to Craig 'Bracko' Brackenridge, Clivo Hillman, Richard Smith, Paskal Millet, David Gamage and all the bands and individuals who kindly gave me their time.

Table of contents:

Foreword.

A good few years back, while cataloguing a large number of vintage scud mags (for a friend), I stumbled upon my collection of Psychobilly fanzines and was immediately transported back to a carefree time of hairspray, cider and returning home from gigs every weekend smelly, battered and knackered. Alan Wilson's 'Deathrow Database' kind of set the bar for the A5 zine as it progressed from a typewritten and photocopied cut 'n' paste job into something far more professional over the years. Undoubtedly the European rockers then took over as we drifted into the next millennium with the heavyweight 'Psychomania' from Germany and Italy's (still-running) 'DogEatRobot'.

In amongst all these publications was issue 7 of 'Short Cuts', which seemed to be based in Sheffield and 'The Crazed'. I must have picked up both of these mags at a gig somewhere as, in the olden days, that was pretty much the only way you could get a hold of this type of creation. Fanzine writers back then were very much in the front-line, whether they were lurking near the backstage doors trying to secure interviews with bands or flogging their wares to a variety of drunken psychos in the gap between sets. Without the ease of Zoom meetings, free Whatsapp calls and email interviews these writers really had to (often literally) get their hands dirty and 'get in there' to secure the copy they required.

It was this intimate interview style that impressed me most about 'The Crazed' because Paul really gave a true flavour not only of the band's themselves but also the circumstances around capturing these conversations such as pressing bands to answer his questions when they were occasionally distracted or grabbing members of other Psychobilly acts as they passed by and throwing a few questions their way as well. I'm sure Paul pestered the life out of a few punters but his style worked and, looking back over all these years, he really captured what the scene was like at the time.

Weirdly, not long after reading my solitary copy of 'The Crazed' I got an email from Paul telling me he was thinking of collecting these long lost interviews together in book form AND in the process of carrying out a series of new interviews to sit alongside the archive material. We eventually met up at Bedlam Breakout and his unmistakeable sense of enthusiasm that those old issues of the zine used to contain still seemed as fresh as it was back then. It's obviously taken a lot of time and effort to create this chunk of Psychobilly history that you now grip firmly in your hands but I believe it has been worth the wait. Get intae it!!

Bracko (March 2023)

Introduction.

Why bother writing a book about The Crazed a Psychobilly/neo-Rockabilly fanzine I produced during the eighties that lasted for four issues. I was even discouraged to write it by a well-known figure on the scene who informed me via email "It's a shame you haven't got more issues as four is not enough for a book". Those not so kindly words did dampen my enthusiasm for a while, but I always thought a book about The Crazed would give a unique perspective of those Psychobilly/Rockabilly, Klub Foot days from the eighties. As I was actually there, interviewing some of the bands at the Klub Foot and asking them about their latest record releases, some of which are now classed as classics within the scene. I interviewed some of the leading bands at the time The Meteors, GuanaBatz, Demented Are Go and Restless to name a few, I met many legendary characters, some who are sadly no longer with us.

The Crazed wasn't looking back at the scene with a retrospective view it was reporting on what was happening at the time. There was a real momentum then as many records were being released on labels such as Nervous Records and ID Records. Bands were experimenting and pushing the Psychobilly/Rockabilly sound forward. The Klub Foot in Hammersmith was the mecca of all things Psychobilly, once or twice The Crazed was sold outside it, although I was more interested in watching or meeting the bands than walking around the venue trying to sell the fanzine. The Crazed was my entry into the scene, hopefully this book will explain the story behind the fanzine and my motivation for producing it and what it all meant to me during the eighties.

At the time the music press virtually ignored Psychobilly and Rockabilly, they certainly didn't seem interested in interviewing bands such as the GuanaBatz or Restless, occasionally the music paper Sounds would review a record or interview one of the more established bands such as The Meteors. This frustrated a teenage me as I was inquisitive and wanted to know more about all the bands.

This frustration gave me the impetus to start The Crazed and interview them myself. There was nothing to intellectualize about it was all about enjoying the music and having a good time. It was a working-class phenomenon that was being mostly ignored by the mainstream even though large numbers of fans turned up regularly at the Klub Foot and bought enough of these bands' records for some of them to gain respectable chart positions within the UK Independent charts. All of this showed that that this youth subculture although ignored could not be silenced. I wanted The Crazed to help give it a voice however small the contribution would be.

Would The Crazed have existed with the advent of the internet? The internet takes away the hunger the bands once had to gain exposure through interviews or reviews. Today, The Crazed might have been a website or a YouTube channel maybe even a Facebook page but with the abundance of information on the internet it might not have needed to happen.

This book is a not a history of Psychobilly and doesn't even attempt to be, it is a look back at a time when I was a teenager and the most important thing on my mind was the next Klub Foot date or when my latest order of vinyl from Raucous Records mail order was going to turn up. The interviews are mostly reproduced as they were published at the time, written quickly and enthusiastically by a teenage me. It is a journey back into a Psychobilly/rockin' world when there was no internet or mobile phones. It is a snapshot from a period which has gone forever, when music and fashion ruled youth culture and you could still shock by your appearance. Step back into my time machine, all the way back to the rockin' eighties.

The Beginning.

In the early eighties Two Tone was just about to breath its last breath, Punk was going underground. The age of the New Romantics was emerging, bands such as Spandau Ballet, Visage and Duran Duran started to appear. Margaret Thatcher was in power, the dole queues were getting longer. Kids leaving school were being thrown onto the Youth Training Scheme, not learning anything just merely doing the crummiest jobs that no one else wanted to do. The Tory backing press demonised the striking Miners. Yuppies and Filofaxes were the trendy terms bringing in the me me me generation. Community spirit was disappearing fast, society was becoming more and more influenced with consumerism. Unlike today there was no internet, Playstations, XBoxes or multi-TV channels, the only escape from these oppressive bleak times was through music and fashion. As a youth what you wore and listened to defined who you were.

Within these rather confusing times I was getting ready to leave school. Like most teenagers I needed to establish an identity, I had no interest in mainstream fashion or the latest bands of the day topping the charts. Why follow the top forty like everyone else and dress and look the same? I remember a group of school friends who were huddled together discussing the merits of the latest Heaven 17 album, how could that music be personal to me? how could it express my teenage angst when I knew everyone else had it. I needed to find something different, not pretentious, or obscure just a movement I could comfortably express myself within. I had previously been a fan of Two Tone having proudly worn a red Harrington jacket, Fred Perry top and a cherished pair of tonic trousers, but that had been when I was eleven years old, times had moved on, crops were being grown out replaced by the dreadful wedge haircut. ABC's Lexicon of Love album was replacing The Specials albums on the nation's turntables. The mainstream seemed to be turning its back on working class street culture, favouring bands whose promotional videos showed success and wealth, hardly relevant to working class youth coming to terms with their overactive hormones and unemployment.

I had first heard Rockabilly music after being bought one of the cheap Pickwick Records compilation albums which the fondly missed high street store Woolworths used to stock, it featured such legends as Warren Smith, Billy Lee Riley and Carl Perkins. The music had a simplicity and edge to it and led to many a happy childhood moment listening to whatever other Rockabilly albums Woolworths would stock. As I approached my teenage years I needed something more contemporary, although I loved the music it was not current I needed music being made now, something I could relate to. It's hardly impressive to try to chat a girl up when you're a teenager by telling her you own the complete Sun Records recordings of Roy Orbison.

Rockabilly music had also been entering the charts with bands such as the Stray Cats, The Polecats and The Jets. These bands were good, but I wanted something with a bit more edge and nastiness to it, music that wouldn't be played on daytime radio. Love Makes the World Go Round by The Jets had no rawness to it, it was smooth, poppy and perfectly played, I didn't feel like a perfect teenager I didn't expect my music to sound like it either.

Within the town centre a new breed of youth culture started appearing, kids with spikey quiffs and shaved sides, wearing t-shirts with images of Frankenstein playing the double bass. I was intrigued and thought they looked like the coolest and most mysterious creatures on the planet. One vivid memory I have is of three of them with their dark quiffs and baseball jackets strutting along the high street blasting out some really cool music from their ghetto blaster which I later I found out was by a band called Restless. Was this the movement I was looking for? I needed to explore further. There was a kid at school with a flat top, we soon became friends, I started to question him about what music he listened to, only to find out he knew absolutely nothing, it was the image not the music for him. I was not to be deterred by this disaster and decided to spend some hard-earned pocket money on an album by a band called The Meteors who were splattered across many t-shirts. I went to the local record shop The Longplayer with my money clenched firmly into my fist and walked straight up to the Rock 'n' Roll section not fully understanding how this one purchase would affect my teenage years. As my fingers flipped through the numerous record sleeves (which in the days of vinyl was really exciting and was sadly lost with the arrival of CDs) I came across the album Wreckin' Crew by The Meteors, I stared at the sleeve looking at the three threatening figures with their quiffs, donkey jackets and a menacing baseball bat, they looked tougher and harder than any band my schoolmates were listening to. My £3.99 flew out of my hand and I rushed home to listen to the album. As soon as the needle hit the vinyl and the manic laughing started at the beginning of the song Insane, I was hooked, this was great it was crude, heavy, rockin' and real it was what I wanted. The Meteors were like a revelation to me, the spirit of fifties Rock 'n' Roll and Rockabilly was there but with something harder, nastier and more current, this was my introduction to Psychobilly music. I ventured back into the record shop and discovered more bands such as The Sting-Rays, GuanaBatz and The Vibes whose crazy version of The Outcasts I'm in Pittsburgh (and it's Raining) was even championed by legendary Radio One DJ John Peel and was named Single of the Week by Sounds a popular music paper. The music was exciting and fresh and was developing with every new release. Punk, Psychedelia and Rockabilly were musical styles all getting thrown into the mix, every band emerging at the time seemed to have a different take and definition of the sound. Whether it was the exotic mixture of garage punk, Psychedelia and Rockabilly of The Sting- Rays and The Vibes or the mixture of Punk and Rockabilly of The Richochets and the GuanaBatz, every release seemed to open another door into the possibilities of the future direction the music could take.

Certain record labels such as Big Beat Records, ID/ABC Records and Nervous Records released this music and became trusted purveyors of taste, you put your faith into their judgement and eagerly allowed them to take your pocket money in exchange for their latest release. There was no YouTube or Spotify to check out the music, often your first taste of the band was when the needle touched the vinyl. I don't recall being let down once. It was a great feeling becoming part of this subculture that the mainstream was mostly unaware of. I remember going into my local Our Price record shop and ordering the Big Beat Records compilation album Rockabilly Psychosis and the Garage Disease the girl serving me thought that I had made the name up, I soon proved her wrong by showing her a review or advert of the album in ZigZag music magazine. It felt good.

I now needed to cultivate the image, I needed to start with my hair, nothing too outrageous or difficult to style to start with. I searched through all the record sleeves and music papers I could to find the right cut, finally finding a photo of The Clash's bassist Paul Simonon sporting a cool flat top. Off I went photo in hand to my local barber only to see a look of horror on their faces. "Oh, Nick's the only one here who can cut that style" I was told whilst being ushered over to an unsuspecting Nick, who upon looking at the photo started to work on my locks. It wasn't perfect but it was a start, it turned a few heads as it wasn't yet a common look then. "I bet you could land an aeroplane on there" some would be comedian said. Upon returning home and looking in the mirror I felt an element of shock at the sudden change of image and a feeling of excitement as I had taken the first step into looking like a Psychobilly. I felt like throwing myself 100% into the scene and the image, other music seemed to pale in comparison, other looks and fashions seemed dull compared to it. My teenage insecurities were getting hidden behind this large juggernaut called Psychobilly that was becoming my world. A blue baseball jacket was purchased at the local market and a King Kurt t-shirt was ordered. I was on my way.

A couple of mates had also grown quiffs since leaving school, Jason was a big Elvis fan and Phil was into the Stray Cats, neither had yet entered into the murky world of Psychobilly! Jay owned a Zephyr Zodiac and I remember briefly driving around with The Milkshakes cover of the Vince Taylor classic Brand New Cadillac blasting out the open windows, which Phil persuaded Jay to play continuously, which after a while got a bit tedious. There was a local Rock 'n' Roll gig coming up, a local band called Red Hot were playing, we decided to go. That night we all bundled into Jay's Zodiac; The Milkshakes yet again being played. Off we went passing all the squares as we drove on. We soon noticed a couple of rockin' folk as we got closer to the venue, we pulled the car over to ask for directions and offer a lift, in they got and off we went. One of them later gained a bit of fame by starring in Dennis Potter's Channel Four television series Lipstick on your Collar she was Louise Germaine. When we got to the venue, we all coolly walked in quiffs held high. It was a mixture of Rockabilly's, Teddy Boys and a couple of Psychobilly's. I remember the hippest people were on the left-hand side standing against the wall, quiffs styled to perfection hair graduated perfectly on their sides. This was the local rockin' scene. We were obviously getting checked out, but you don't go and introduce yourself, you are just there getting seen, letting people see your face. In time I got to know a lot of people there but at this moment I was an unknown.

King Kurt.

A lot of the bands put their contact addresses on the back of their record sleeves for fans to write to, I sent off many a stamped addressed envelope waiting to see what information or goodies (badges, photos) might be returned. I wrote to King Kurt who had recently had a top forty hit and a television appearance on the UK's top music show Top of the Pops. I received a biography of the band which supplied me with the following details, which are mostly total nonsense but entertaining nonetheless:

King Kurt the Rat was born in March 1984, on a cold dark night in a blind alley off the Old Kent Road. His father died of self-abuse a few days earlier and his mother fled to New York. He was set upon by a group of Tom Cats. Just he and his brother Horatio survived from a family of eleven. He vowed for vengeance. Kurt emerged in Brixton and observed the humans obsessed by Cats (Stray Cats, Polecats etc). He then recruited six people John, Boppin' Bert, Smeg, Rory, Thwack and Maggot and when they played their sound drove out every Cat. In the Summer of 1982, they released their first single Zulubeat to teach the Rats to dance the Ooh Wallah Wallah, the ancient celebration of Rat supremacy. They signed to Stiff in September 1983-Destination Zululand.

Rory Lyons the drummer of King Kurt also sent me a handwritten letter concerning my interest in joining their Rat and Rodent Club.

"Paul. Thanks for writing in, here's your R'nR Club Card. We're not quite sure what it'll get you but if you bring it to one of our gigs you'll get in cheaper. We're making an LP at the moment, guaranteed to be more horrible than anything you've heard yet. It might be called Ooh Wallah Wallah but we're not sure yet (sure about a lot of things aren't we!). Thanks Rory"

I was impressed to have direct contact with an established band. It allowed me to understand that although I didn't live in London or attend loads of gigs, I could still be aware of what was happening and feel part of the scene. To integrate myself further I decided to cobble together some ropey drawings of King Kurt I had done and create a few cartoons featuring members of the band, then staple all my efforts together to resemble a comic/fanzine which I named Kurtzine and send it to Rory. Much to my surprise I received a postcard from Spain from him and later a three-sided letter.

"What a brilliant comic you sent. It must have taken ages. We've all had a good look at it and think it's great especially Maggot because he's the mastermind on good comics" he wrote. "We've got a new record out in two weeks Banana Banana it's a sort of Tarzan calypso thingy and I really like it, but I would. Evil John and Sickface Bert wanted to do something different so they've left but it's all for the best because it's hard to do anything with people who aren't 100% committed to it. There are strong rumours that Smeggy's bought a ....Cat. He bought it paid real money for a Cat, we're all stunned by the news, but maybe he's only bought it to wash the dishes with.

We went to Finland a couple of weeks ago. It was really good. We played a couple of festivals out there, one with twenty people, the other with about two thousand people. Smeggy was his usual disgusting self and we all had a good laugh. It doesn't get dark out there in the Summer, so we just sat around drinking all day and day!!

I'm going to Wales for a week to learn how to fly hawks, real wacky that eh, but I don't think they'll let me keep one in Brixton.

Well, that's about it, look after yourself keep doing the comic it's great."

I never expected such a long, friendly, and informative reply, my poorly drawn but enthusiastic comic had obviously entertained him and the band. In the next few months more Kurtzines were sent and more replies from Rory received. Here are highlights taken from his letters and postcards:

"Thanks for the latest instalment of 'My Quiff is my Strength' (a cartoon I had created for the Kurtzine). I really enjoyed it, really funny and so did everyone else who's seen it."

"Smeg and Paul are off to somewhere in the middle of nowhere to write some new songs and search for mushrooms and Maggots somewhere but probably very drunk."

"Yesterday we did a telly thingy with Bananarama, but it's for cable TV so unless you move to Swindon, you'll probably never see it but nor will I so that makes it equal. We had to throw bananas at them (original huh!) and generally annoy everybody, which wasn't very hard."

"It's really hard to settle down after me holiday. I stayed for two weeks it was that good and had a brilliant time chasing Magpies and generally going mad. Magpie chasing is really good, they ought to have it at the Olympics. I knew they were useful for something, but I never knew what. You chase the Magpies into a bush or tree and then send the Hawk up and then beat hell out of the bush, so they fly out and get boshed by the Hawk. It sounds simple but it isn't that easy 'cos Magpies are quite clever, so they don't fly out or they go down Rabbit holes! I've got Buzzard footprints all up my arm where one of them got a bit friendly."

"Stiff Records made a balls up and didn't put Banana Banana Banana Banana on the twelve inch, they put the same Banana Banana as the seven inch on it, so if you haven't got it, I wouldn't bother"

"Sorry it isn't very long but I'm not feeling very intellectual today."

"We're out here (Spain) doing the usual things, hotel wrecking, van crashing, nothing spectacular, just expensive. Mack the Knife's out 16th April (1984), it's a different version, much better."

"The only trouble with being an artist is you don't make any money until you're dead."

"If anyone offers you any money to go to Amsterdam, don't go it's full of dogs and bikes."

"Well, King Kurt goes to Hollywood, but at least we won't get Aids!!"

"We buggered off to Germany for a fortnight tour in late

September, with Normal Norman a borrowed guitarist who ended up Abnormal Norman and Neil a very old bass player. It was great, very grubby, lots of Frauleins and highly successful, so successful that we came back with a £3000 bill for hotel squashing. We had nutty parties every night and the last one got a bit out of hand, so the Fire Brigade and Police kept coming, hence the bill. Anyway, this bankrupted us, honestly, so we all signed on when we got back."

"Paul's been working hard so now we've got about twelve new songs to do and rehearse and then record and if Stiff like them we'll get some wages again, that'll be a relief. (these songs became the Big Cock album). I've been painting and decorating for a month to get some money."

"It looks like we might have a new bass player Henry Mackenzie, a ready-made Zulu. He's a friend from a few years back and we're breaking him in gently. We're having a bit of trouble finding a new guitarist, but I'm sure one'll turn up. We should have started playing last week but Paul's got Housemaids Knee so he's got to lie in bed with his leg in the air for a week! I've been playing drums for the Blubbery Hellbellies and that's good fun."

"I went to Wales this week for a few days out catching Rabbits with Fred the Goshawk and that was great. I'm going back in a couple of weeks."

"Smeg's got a black eye, he and our old singer Jeff got in a fight at a gig in Brighton and they both got a black eye each. Smeg got boshed at The Meteors not long ago too."

"The Rock Around the Clock thing was great fun, (it was a marathon television and radio extravaganza aired by the BBC in 1984) I got pissed and was sick on the BBC's steps outside!"

"I'm working tonight behind the bar at the Academy in Brixton. It's Yellowman tonight. Last time he played the crowd tried to raid the bar with teargas, so I hope it's quieter this time. I used to work at the bar in the 101 Club where we used to play a lot and really enjoy it, it's fun watching everyone get drunk."

"We're back on Stiff (Records) which was a big shock to them and us, but I reckon it's the only place suitable!"

I also received an unexpected Christmas card signed by the band. I realised through these letters and postcards that a fan could open up a line of communication. The first seeds of creating my own fanzine were sown.

The Idea.

In the back pages of the music press, fanzines were sometimes advertised or mentioned. Once purchased a fanzine would promote others creating a domino effect. This was a totally home-grown industry and had no rules or regulations, they were written by fans and read by fans. They could be as professional or amateurish as they wanted, sometimes typed out or on occasion written by hand. You could often read about bands not always championed by the music press or discover up and coming bands. The interviews or reviews did not always have to be written in a coherent structure, but they were always full of passion and enthusiasm for the subject matter. I remember Billy Bragg mentioning an interview wherein he was questioned about Subbuteo. In these pre internet days if a band or style of music wasn't played on the radio or written about in the music press, the chance of hearing it was virtually non-existent, fanzines offered that lifeline, although often to a very limited readership. The philosophy of fanzines wasn't about making money, it was to share your passion and love for the music. They were made and written from the heart. Profit was not a factor, it was often lost or put into the costs of the next issue. Some fanzines such as Sniffin' Glue have become legendary, capturing a moment in time, preserving it in the yellowing xeroxed pages in people's collections today.

I needed to find out more about Psychobilly, what made the bands tick? what were they like, what were their views and influences. What strove and drove these individuals to create and sustain this scene that I was throwing myself into. I was too curious to just have a great record collection, I wanted to know who made the records and why. You could read many an article discussing the merits and influence of The Clash and the Sex Pistols but who was speaking to and trying to understand the music of GuanaBatz or The Sting-Rays?

54321 was a fanzine I discovered in the back pages of some mainstream music publication (the name of which is lost in my distant memories). It featured interviews with The Sting-Rays and The Vibes. My 15p plus stamped addressed envelope was eagerly sent to an address in Ealing, London. It arrived a few days later (13p postage). It was great, the interviews gave me a real open window into what seemed a far and distant world. Yes, I had a direct link to King Kurt but you couldn't expect other bands to have Rory's openness. Anyway, I didn't want to sit around all day writing letters and drawing cartoons. The Sting-rays interview within the fanzine was great and gave me more of an insight into the band, even though the batteries of the cassette recorder ran out during the interview and Chris P (who ran the fanzine) had to write it mostly based on what he remembered. I learnt the following information, Bal the singer worked for Big Beat Records as a stock controller. Double bass player MK left to continue his medical studies. Bal wanted their first album deleted as he thought there were too many fillers on the album and that the band didn't do the songs justice. Alec the drummer wrote most of the lyrics and that initial pressings of the first album came with a lyric sheet. Bal stated that he liked The Prisoners, The Vibes (who he used to manage) and The X Men who he wished would rehearse more. Bal also stated that he had drawn the cover of the Rockabilly Psychosis and the Garage Disease compilation album and helped to compile it. The Vibes interview was just as revealing and featured direct quotes as Chris had bought new batteries. A surprise fact was that Boz Boorer former Polecats guitarist was in an early line up. Other revelations included the band disliking the cover of their Can You Feel? ep "it was a bit of a flop" said singer Gary Boniface. The band had actually split up due to clashes with each other but later agreed to reform. Their influences were the 60's garage sound, with a '76 Punk sound along with elements of Rockabilly and the Blues. They also had a song called Constipation Blues and a gig had resulted in half the band getting arrested. These interviews and the style of the fanzine inspired me to seriously consider starting my own. To be able to meet and interview my favourite bands seemed a very exciting prospect and would allow me to attempt to make a name for myself within the scene.

I sent a rather ropey drawing of a Skeleton led Psychobilly band to Chris P who very kindly and probably out of a little pity featured it in issue two as the background image for an article about a

Psychobilly band called The Bloodstains. Chris had also been present at the legendary Four on Four recording for Channel Four's seminal Friday night music show The Tube which featured The Sting-Rays, TallBoys, Thee Milkshakes and The Prisoners. "I saw myself on tv down the front for The Sting-Rays. It was quite funny though 'cos all the bands were miming. It was a laugh but on tv it didn't present the bands to their best really during the interview bit" he wrote to me.

I got a job in the warehouse at a local furniture factory to help fund my growing obsession. I met a Rockabilly there who was about my age and looked and dressed like he would listen to The Meteors or GuanaBatz but unfortunately didn't. After work we rushed back to his home to listen to some rockin' tunes. He had bought a Gene Vincent album through a dealer in Record Collector magazine but was not impressed with the condition of the vinyl and decided to send it back for a refund. I wanted to listen to some Psychobilly, but he wasn't interested, he said it was too punky and a bit of a racket! I stayed for a couple of hours much to my parent's dismay as my dinner had long gone cold, they thought I had disappeared off the face of the earth. I later lent him a copy of The Milkshakes album 20 Rock n Roll Greats, his (also rockin') girlfriend never forgave me! needless to say it was returned pretty promptly. I remember he once tried to take on a whole gang of casuals outside a popular nightclub after a night of drinking. He introduced me to a few other rockin' folk a couple of whom I remembered at the Red Hot gig. One of them Rod had a brother who was the singer for a Psychobilly band called Skitzo.

Once I got introduced to these local rockin' folks and started discussing the merits of The Meteors and GuanaBatz the more I felt part of the scene and not just an observer. Every day we were hanging around the local cafes making a cup of tea last an hour, walking around town, checking our quiffs in the reflections of shop windows. If it rained, we promptly ducked for cover, nothing could ruin our pristine quiffs. I remember us all walking out of the local Our Price record shop and one of the lads who I had went to see Red Hot with just looked at us open mouthed. We felt the real deal, we weren't a gang, we were members of a youth culture with different interests and values than the mainstream, we were cool.

I had bought an American airman's style leather jacket and went out proudly wearing it. After a night out with a mate Charlie, we begun making our way back from the pub when I decided to use what I thought was a shortcut. Making sure he was following me I shouted out: "Follow me Charlie" and then landed feet first standing upright waist deep in a small waterfall that I had forgotten about in my alcoholic state. Charlie burst into constant hysterics during the long and very wet walk home. The jacket was ruined. I certainly wasn't the coolest in the group. Not everyone was accepted into the group, a lad was told by a rather tough Ted whom we all knew to do a Basil Fawlty style walk outside a cafe, which he obediently did, but he still wasn't welcome to stay. I also remember him pulling a knife out of his jacket in our local cafe to try to impress us much to everybody's shock and disgust, not cool. One gig we attended was in a local pub and featured a band called Rocket 88, who played more traditional Rockabilly and Rhythm and Blues. A group of Punks entered the pub, including one who used to be a Psychobilly. One of them, who was on a visit from New Zealand stood in front of the lead singer Leroy and drunkenly stared at him whilst he was performing, Leroy was not deterred and continued singing. I later found that after the gig one of the Teds in the audience decided to teach the Punk a lesson in manners, with a chain.

The Unknown.

Rod and a lad called Graham Smurf Murphy decided to form a band called The Unknown. Rod had been in a band in London with his brother Phil and Smurf had been practising the guitar for a while and was now pretty good. Rod's brother-in-law Charlie played drums. They rehearsed in Rod's other brother in law's house and for one of the rehearsals I was asked to take photos. Rod knew how to pose for the camera as he slapped his double bass, whilst Charlie gazed out of the window drumming up a beat, Smurf did not want to be photographed at all and sat uncomfortably on a chair strumming whilst I snapped away. Charlie was quickly replaced by a lad called Steve who had a full drum set. One night the band were rehearsing in a basement of a local cafe. Rod had a headache and asked if someone could fetch him some painkillers, I agreed and walked up the stairs and opened a door that led into the kitchen, a rather large Alsatian appeared from behind the door and looked at me. The next moment this seemingly docile dog growled and jumped up baring his teeth. Miraculously I managed to run out into the cafes backyard and quickly pushed a bin against the door, all the time hearing the dog's demonic bark. The band were oblivious to all this commotion going on above their heads and continued to rehearse. I alarmingly looked at my arm now sporting two bloody bite marks. I was stuck out there with just a bin between me and a dog that had just tasted my blood. It seemed like an eternity being stuck in the backyard; I couldn't escape as the owners had put shards of glass along the top of the wall to deter intruders. After about ten minutes the band stopped playing and there was complete silence, the only noise was the dog barking. The son of the owner of the cafe mercifully returned to find me standing in his backyard holding my freshly bitten arm "Jesus" I remember him saying. The dog was now safely hidden away. We decided to descend the stairs into the basement to see if the very silent band were still there, when he opened the basement door there was no one to be seen, until the band slowly started to appear from behind boxes and curtains. They looked shocked to see me standing in front of them and explained their horror listening to the dog barking and prowling around above them, they thought that I had been the dog's dinner. Drummer Steve's girlfriend quickly drove me to the hospital, where my wound was cleaned, and I received a tetanus jab from a mildly amused nurse. I still have a scar today from one of the bites.

The Unknown managed to secure a gig supporting Rod's brothers' band Skitzo in Chatham, a minibus was hired, we all paid to travel with the band to show our support. Whilst waiting in a car park for the vehicle to arrive, one of the girls in the entourage accidently sprayed her rather large quiff with deodorant instead of hairspray. The band set up whilst we ordered drinks from the bar. During the gig the band played well, one song I remember them performing was a self-penned song called Playground which I liked, and which was dedicated to me. A local Ted was bopping away in front of them obviously appreciating the band much to Rod's annoyance who labelled him Elvis. Rod's brother Phil and his band Skitzo then came onto the stage, it was the first time I had seen or heard them. They were very good, soon to be signed up to Nervous Records and releasing their debut album Skitzo Mania. The Unknown's debut gig had been a success. Unfortunately, the band seemed to drift apart and never performed again. Smurf started to play with more traditional Rockabilly and Rhythm and Blues bands. Rod laid down his double bass and eventually joined Skitzo many,many years later. Steve the drummer, I have no idea what happened to him.

The Crazed starts to emerge.

Now, I thought was the time to start my own fanzine. I liked the Punk do it yourself attitude and I had no interest in making money or producing a sleek glossy publication. Meeting the bands was my main priority. I tried to find as many band addresses as I could from record sleeves, I remember Nervous Records compilation album Hell's Bent on Rockin' had a few printed on the inner sleeve. I sent off quite a few letters with stamped addressed envelopes asking for interviews with the bands. I even asked Rory from King Kurt if the band would be up for an interview. I waited and waited for the replies to come flying through my letterbox, the only problem, none did, even Rory never mentioned an interview in his reply to yet another dodgy Kurtzine. This major setback didn't deter me I was still determined to interview the bands and why shouldn't I? I was bubbling over with enthusiasm and couldn't wait to start firing questions off to them, unanswered letters wouldn't stop me. I contacted Chris P of 54321 fanzine who was very encouraging and sent two gig reviews, the first was The Vibes at Dingwalls, London and the second was The Surfadelics a Mod style Garage band at The Clarendon, Hammersmith:

The Vibes.

...Ah, those greeny, browny, groovy Vibes. Wait, wait, let me think...oh forget it let me dance. Yes, yes, I've found my feet and they appear to be twisting, jumping and stomping...No one can lick Johnny J's rhythms, Gary has a scream to rival the Ledge and Hase Adkins, Bob out fuzzes Johnny Mthr' Johnstone, who in turn turns out to be one of the wild men of well, good Rock, while Lloyd is simply bigger than anybody else on double bass... Hey, hey what's this sand dance-it must be that Egyptian Thing to blame. Are you lookin' out for the Judgement Day or are you already Lookin' In A Mirror. I'm Mad but Scratch My Back just the same will you. Now get out of my way or you may find yourself Inside Out with the Mini Skirt Blues... Those psychotic punksters sure know how to knock 'em dead. How about tracking down their two singles and their LP, when it's released? No, don't argue just do it, The Vibes are worth it...

The Surfadelics.

Although the surf may not be too good in Stratford, East London, this is where The Sufadelics hail from. The Thames is a ten-minute walk from the Clarendon as well, but The Surfadelics still create waves. Dickydelic, Barrydelic, Kennydelic, Tonydelic and Martydelic produce a tight "fab fun" pop sound with its roots in the sixties but with most of their ditties actually being self-penned. Their contribution to Garage Goodies and their single Too Good To Be True set the tone, but there are plenty more mod(dern), pop(ular) garage (class) hits where they came from to set your body moving or your toes a tapping at least.

Chris P informed me about a "bloke called Paul Jones, who is putting together a compilation tape of Rockabilly, Psychobilly and Garage Trash bands!" who hailed from Banbury Oxon. Chris was going to send him a rough demo tape of his band The Moonsters and told me that The Sting-Rays and X-Men had shown an interest. Paul was looking for a name for the compilation tape and in my ever-enthusiastic manner I sent him a list of proposed titles and some ropey drawings. He responded: "Thanks for the designs and names, I'm going to probably use the Trashe design and call it Psycho Holocaust after Garage Holocaust gave me the idea, thanks". The drawings I sent him have long ago been filed away in the bin. He planned on placing an advert in Sounds for bands. Two months later during July 1985 I received a letter from Paul stating: "I've had a lack of support from groups, so far I've only got three - The Bloodstains, The Moonsters and The Toads, I'm trying to find more bands". I never heard from Paul again, at least it wasn't just me getting frustrated with the lack of response.

I needed a new tactic to get the bands to respond to me, requesting face to face interviews wasn't working, they didn't know me, and I didn't know them, I also didn't have any previous examples of any articles or interviews to show. I was basically an anonymous person requesting to meet and interview them for a fanzine that they had never heard of. Why should they bother? I was enthusiastic to interview them, maybe they weren't keen on being interviewed, possibly the music said all they wanted to say. I decided to compile a list of questions to send to the bands, if they wouldn't meet me maybe they would respond to these. It wasn't what I had initially wanted but if they responded at least I would have some kind of interview. Failure was not an option! With no previous experience I had to think up a list of questions for the bands I would choose to contact. I approximately came up with eight questions, they were mostly really standard questions such as -when were you formed, who are your influences and who does most of the song writing, nothing challenging or controversial. So, more stamps were bought, my questionnaires were sent, now the tense waiting game begun. After a little time, the responses began to arrive, it was an exciting time even though most of the answers were as brief as my questions. Some of the replies included telephone numbers which gave me direct access to these bands, things were moving along well. I rang Mike Lister from The Wigsville Spliffs who had kindly completed one of my questionnaires he informed me that The Crazed was generating interest and discussion from the bands.

Issue 1.

Eventually I received completed questionnaires from Torment, The Wigsville Spliffs, Nervous Records supremo Roy Williams and The Pharaohs. I realised that The Crazed needed to feature more than these rather short interviews. I decided to review a few records and included the following reproduced verbatim:

Restless: The Early Years 1981-1983 (Album on Nervous Records)

A collection of previously unreleased 'early Restless' recordings, released on the bands original record label Nervous Records. After listening to the latest Restless album 'After Midnight' it was good to hear Restless rockin' it up again on this collection of previously unreleased tracks from the early days of Restless. The LP includes five tracks from the legendary but previously unreleased demo tape Restless sent Nervous who after five seconds decided to sign them up. Anyway, the very fresh sounding Restless rock up a few old classics such as Twenty Flight Rock, Rock The Joint etc, along with the original version of Hightime, these tracks were recorded live in the studio to sound just like how Restless would play them live at the time but did they use a piano in their original live act? if you listen carefully to Rock The Joint you can just about make one out, who is this mysterious pianist? or is Mark Harman playing it with his feet? whilst he's playing guitar and singing at the same time and do remember this has been recorded live so there's no overdubs. Anyway, these five vintage Restless tracks are great to have in your record collection, I only wish I could hear more from this original session. The next few tracks on the album are taken from the bands two Nervous LP's 'Why Don't You Just Rock' and 'Do You Feel Restless?' but to carry on the previously unreleased policy of the album they've been remixed by the bands contemporary producer Pete Gage who also produced the Klub Foot LP's and various other acts on ID and ABC Records, fortunately he hasn't done any 12" disco remixes on any of the tracks, he's kept all the songs in their original form but changing the production around making it clearer and also bringing certain instruments out which were previously kept in the background, in all he's done a pretty good job on the tracks. I think it was a bit of a dodgy idea but fortunately it came over well on this record. The last three tracks are taken from the bands Edge on You single session and it actually includes the original mix of the classic Nervous single and I can't understand how tracks as good as Why Didn't I Stay At Home? and Slidin' On Down The Hill can stay unreleased for three years it makes you wonder how many more classic tracks are locked in the Nervous vaults. If you enjoyed the two LPs Restless released on Nervous then this is for you or if you enjoy modern Rockabilly then give this LP a listen you won't be disappointed.

Archie: Listen to What Archie Says (Mini L.P. on Kix 4U Records.)

I don't know much about this band except that they come from the same country as the almighty Batmobile, Holland. This is an eight-track mini-L.P. and obviously there are a few comparisons to Batmobile, but that's not to say that Archie haven't got their own sound though. The L.P. starts off with the brilliant title track Listen to What Archie Says played at frantic speed. As this is on Kix 4 U Records (a division of Europe's Rockhouse label) the production throughout is clear, due to the fact that the infamous Bert Rockhuizen produced it. Things slow down a bit for the next two tracks, but both don't fail to disappoint. Then to finish side one is the crazy Steel Cap Stomp. Side two starts off with Radar Love but it sounds nothing like The Pharaohs version of the song this version is a faster version. The other tracks on side two keep up the frantic pace. The L.P. comes to a close with the instrumental In Search of (The Lost Prairie Oysters) which although not being a classic song keeps up with the frantic pace of the rest of the songs on the L.P. This band has got a lot of potential and maybe with a bit more experience could well become as popular as Batmobile over Europe (maybe even more?).

Rochee and The Sarnos: Rumble in the Jungle (7" single on Nervous Records)

The crazy, insane Rochee and The Sarnos, yes you know that band who released the sensitive, gentle Understanding Sarno L.P. with such deeply moving songs such as Understanding Croissants, Rochee is a Monster etc. Here is a Sarno 45 released on Nervous Records two tracks in all. The A side is Rumble in the Jungle, with a spoken vocal throughout the song, I think it must have been recorded in a padded cell, what with Rochee telling us about the inhabitants of the Jungle with names such as Oogallo, Sprungel etc, typical Rochee madness. The B side is just as strange it's called Whistle Wriggle and that's really just what it is., Rochee whistling along with the band, really there's only one word to describe this single...CRAZY.

These were pretty favourable reviews that contained very little critical analysis. The fanzine was my chance to promote the scene and show publicly my appreciation for it. To criticise a band or a record seemed pointless to me at the time. If I didn't like something why include it in my fanzine? I had no wish to antagonize bands, fans or record labels, I was trying to promote them all (myself included) in a positive way. I was a fan writing to and for other fans, I had no axe to grind and no huge ego waiting to be unleashed. What could be worse than trying to stop someone buying a record or following a band by a few harsh words written by me? Maybe it was the wrong direction to take, but that was my teenage opinion.

I was keen on understanding the musical influences of the bands I was featuring and thought the best way to do it was to ask the bands to compile their favourite top ten records. It was also a great way of adding interesting additional content. The top ten list I included in issue one was by an up-and-coming neo-Rockabilly band called Fractured (details of how I obtained their lists will be revealed later).

Fractured top tens.

Mike Herman: Rhythm Guitar.

Elvis-Teddybear.

Dave Phillips and the Hot Rod Gang-Wild Youth.

AC/DC-Hell Ain't a Bad Place to Be.

Stray Cats-Rock this Town.

Tony Crombie and his Rockets-Sticks and Stones.

Restless-Ice Cold.

Slim Harper-Shake Your Hips.

The Jets-Jitterbug Baby.

Bill Haley-Happy Baby.

Bill Haley-I Still Love You All.

Paul Everdell: Vocals, Lead Guitar.

Tommy Steele-This is No Build Up.

Bill Haley-Real Rock Drive

Eddie Cochran-Twenty Flight Rock

Rod Willis-The Cat

Andrews Sisters-Don't Sit Under the Apple Tree

Dire Straits-Romeo and Juliet

Little Richard-She's Got It

Gene Vincent-Pink Thunderbird

Eddie Cochran-Am I Blue

Merrille Moore-King Porter Stomp

Nick Hoadley:Bass

Carol Lynn and The Musical Twins-Rockin' Out the Blues

The Vibes-Pretty Baby

Jerry Lee Lewis-The Wild One

Ric Carty-I Want You to Know

Benny Joy-Miss Bobby Sox

Little Richard-Ooh my Soul

Joe Clay-You Look That Good to Me

Thurston Harris-Be Bop a Leba

Hasil Adkins-Truley Ruley

The Sabres-Take Up the Slack Daddy O

Paul 'Squit' Davies:Drums

Grieg-Piano Concerto

The Meteors-Hills Have Eyes

Dion and the Belmonts-The Wanderer

Phil Collins-In the Air Tonight

Glen Miller-Moonlight Serande

Queen-Bohemian Rhapsody

Gershwin-Rhapsody in Blue

Alison Moyet-Ole Devil called Love

Communards-Don't Slip Away

Dire Straits-Sultans of Swing

Some of the choices such as Dire Straits, Queen and Phil Collins weren't what I was expecting, but it reflected a true indication of the bands musical tastes and now allows us an historical glimpse at what a mid-eighties neo-Rockabilly band listened to.

Outer Limits.

I had received a photograph from a band called Outer Limits who had been featured on the Nervous Records compilation album Hell's Bent on Rockin' they had also included a brief biography and a request for the photograph to be returned after I had used it for publication. It was received a long time before a lot of the other replies and so had been collecting dust. A local secondhand record shop had put me into contact with a local lad who produced his own fanzine which featured his own cartoons and artwork. He introduced me to a friend of his whose father worked or owned a printers and kindly offered to copy the photograph to make it look better when printed/copied, I keenly handed the photo over and never saw him or the photo again. Fortunately, I had photocopied it and later included this far from perfect quality copy in the fanzine. I later explained this to a very forgiving band member Paul Gaskin. The Outer Limits feature included in the fanzine:

Outer Limits hail from Billericay, Essex. With their clever well written songs which include a wide variety of influences played with a Rockabilly beat. They have released an excellent single The Chase and a 12" E.P. Edge of Time, both on Dog Rock Records. They have also had tracks featured on the Nervous Records compilation Hell's Bent on Rockin' and Zorch Factor One. I'll let lead singer and bassist of the band Martin 'Johno' Johnson explain the rest. "We've been together about four years, we started by playing Rockabilly music like Johnny Burnette and Gene Vincent etc, we developed our own sound and songs far from the topics of straight Rockabilly." The band members apart from Johno are Paul Gaskin (guitar) and Rob Tyler on drums. "We have all played for various bands including Dave Phillips 'Hot Rod Gang', Renegade and Dr Ubangi. We have played Germany, Italy etc." and as well Outer Limits have played to enthusiastic audiences around England including the Klubfoot. So, if you haven't seen Outer Limits yet go and see them, they're well worth seeing!

The band had also included tour dates which weren't published in the fanzine as the dates would have already been played before publication. For those of you who are curious they were: Clarendon Hotel (downstairs) Saturday 3rd August 1985, Klub Foot (Meteors) Saturday 10th August 1985 and Klub Foot Saturday 24th August 1985. The band also wished me luck with my "rockin zine".

The Coffin Nails

The Coffin Nails were another band starting to make a name for themselves on the Psychobilly scene. I had obtained lead singer Tony Sjazer's telephone number and after a few deep breaths rang him, he turned out to be a really nice guy and told me that he had just got married, moved and had left the band. I found out that the guitarist of the band Steve 'Humungus' Clarke had taken over lead vocals (which would soon change) and other personal changes. I did not have a proper interview with the band but had enough information for a small article. I had received a photograph of the band posing on a cross by a grave, which gave me an idea on how to write their piece:

It's midnight in the graveyard, the air is dense, the atmosphere is chillingly cold an Owl hoots in the distance breaking the deathly silence that fills the place. I light a cigarette calmly trying not to let my nerves get the better of me, then suddenly a strange light appears from behind three gravestones. I step back in horror, a deathly scream can be heard, there's a flutter of Bat's wings, then when I get the courage to open my eyes three mutated figures are standing in front of me "We are the Coffins Nails" the figures say in unison. "The Coffins Nails?" I reply, "Why you can't be as the Coffins Nails are a fourpiece!" "No longer, our screaming vocalist Tony Sjazer is departing, the daughter of Dracula put her fangs into him, now he's getting hitched to her and moving to Coventry." "Who will scream for the band now?" I ask. "Steve 'Humungus' Clarke our guitarist will twist his vocal cords round." they reply. "So, tell us who's in the band now?" "Well as you know Steve is now vocalist and guitarist and a self-confessed alcoholic, Graham Farr is still on bass and his ambition in life is to be breast fed by a Hippo but Toby Griffin no longer drums for us he was spirited away by The Meteors so we got a replacement in Dave Ward who used to create a thud with a band called Jonah Reece." I was just about to ask another question when all three figures disappeared. I look around the graveyard only to find it just as quiet as it was before this occurrence, in the distance I notice daylight. is emerging I stamp out my cigarette and go back into the world of the living.

This piece of writing whilst far from perfect captures a Psychobilly feel, it is my favourite part of issue one. Toby Griffin former Coffin Nails drummer complimented me by writing "I like the 'interview' with The Coffin Nails, that was a good idea."

Nervous Records.

Nervous Records in my humble opinion helped to fuel the resurgence in Rockabilly music and push the emergence of the then new Psychobilly movement. Nervous a rockin' only record label released classic albums by bands such as The Ricochets, The Deltas, Frenzy and introduced Restless to the record buying public. It's first release in 1979 was Rockabilly Guy by The Polecats who later re-recorded it for Mercury Records and scored a UK top forty hit. Roy Williams the owner of Nervous was always a friendly, helpful and informative person to chat to, I recall many a long phone call to him and he was always worthy of a good chat at the Klub Foot, he would be easy to spot as he would be the only Teddy Boy there. He received a list of questions from me through the post and oddly gave very short precise answers. This is what was printed, with just a little editing to the introduction.

Nervous Records a label that's helped so many Rockin' bands get where they are today. Really this label needs no introduction as any true Rockabilly or Psychobilly would already be familiar with the labels record catalogue. Nervous have been the first label to release records by acts such as Restless, The Polecats, Frenzy, The Deltas, the list is never ending and the label release a numerous number of Rockin' classics. This label is just as important as the bands that are on it.

Here Roy Williams of Nervous answers my questions about his record label.

Q. When was Nervous Records started and by whom?

A. Roy Williams and Stuart Wester started Nervous Publishing to publish The Jets songs when they manged them in 1978. Roy and Stuart were both dj's on The Wild Wax Show.

Q. What was the intention of starting Nervous?

A. To bring Rock 'N' Roll/Rockabilly up to date and re-popularise it.

Q. Do you think you've stuck to your original intensions?

A. Most of the time.

Q. How did you get to sign your first act The Polecats?

A. They wanted a gig at one of my disco gigs.

Q. Did you find it easy releasing the first Nervous Record Rockabilly Guy by The Polecats?

A. No, I didn't have enough money!

Q. How do you feel when you build a band up such as Restless/Frenzy and they go and sign to another label?

A. They go after we discuss it. If another label can pay them an advance and I can't then I tell them to go, although I often assist in the paperwork involved.

Q. What has been the biggest selling Nervous Record?

A. NERD004 (which is the catalogue number to 'Why Don't You Just Rock' by Restless.

Q. Have you got a personal favourite?

A. Buzz and The Flyers.

Q. Are there any records you regret releasing?

A. No.

Q. Why did you delete The Frenzy 'Robot Riot' 12" e.p. when the record is still in demand by those who didn't buy it first time round?

A. It just wasn't selling, I was rather disappointed with its sales because I thought it was very good. Many people rang in to ask but they didn't actually buy it. Anyway, we've gotta have some rarities!

Q. As you've done an Aussiebilly' L.P. are you going to do a similar l.p. on another country?

A. If I like the material enough. (I rang Roy a few weeks after this interview and he was contemplating doing a similar l.p. on American rockin' bands as he had been impressed by the material he had been sent. One band he was extremely impressed by was called The Jackals whom he described as sounding like The Cramps at their best but obviously having a sound of their own, sounds interesting....)

Q. Would you ever release a record which is not either Rockabilly/Rock 'N' Roll?

A. Not on Nervous Records.

Q. As a few of your bands have been featured on compilation videos such as Blood on The Cats/ Stomping At The Klub Foot are Nervous going to release any videos?

A. Not in the foreseeable future. (Although Jettisoundz Video are releasing a Skitzo video to coincide with their Nervous L.P. and a follow up to the Blood on The Cats video which will feature a few Nervous acts, which will probably be called For A Few Pussies More.)

Q. Is there any band which you have not signed which you wish you had?

A. Loads!

Q. What can we expect from Nervous in the future?

A. More from Torment, Get Smart l.p. just released, l.p. from Skitzo (which should be out by the time you get this issue of The Crazed), Zorch Factor Two. Lined up for later on in the year is possible l.p.'s from The Caravan's and The Rhythmaires. (and as I wrote earlier on a possible U.S.A Billy l.p. later on in the year as well.)

The Wigsville Spliffs.

Mike Lister of the The Wigsville Spliffs a great rockin' trio also answered my list of questions, he was a very helpful and friendly bloke to speak to on the phone. I remember one call in which he informed me that word had got around on the scene that my fanzine was starting and it was creating a bit of a buzz, I don't know whether he was just being kind to me, but it did show a true reflection of the lack of interest the national music press showed in these bands at the time. Mike also invited me to a gig The Spliffs were playing at The Klub Foot and told me I would be on their guest list! in my world this was a true honour, it was like receiving the golden ticket. The Wigsville Spliff's criminally never released an l.p. at the time but were featured on various compilation albums, most notably Stomping at The Klub Foot Volume Three which featured a blistering version of their classic 'Al Capone'. Raucous Records later collected all these scattered tracks and released them on an excellent compilation c.d. which I still play today.

Here are the Wigsville Spliffs from issue one:

Having become regulars at the Klub Foot and having built up a solid Wigsivillian following The Wigsville Spliffs have certainly become a name to look out for on the Rockin' circuit. Having appeared on a numerous number of rockin' compilation albums such as Stomping at The Klub Foot Volume Three, James Deans of The Dole Queue, Dance To It etc and also appearing on the Klub Foot video the Spliffs have certainly built up a healthy reputation for themselves. They've also changed their appearance as well, shedding the jeans and t-shirt look for a baseball orientated stage look.

So enough of this introduction here Mike Lister who slaps his bass for the band answers my Wigsvillian questions.

Q. When were The Wigsville Spliffs formed?

A. Mid-year 1984.

Q. Have you always had the same line up?

A. Yes, Ian Aitken vocals and guitar, Mike Lister (me) bass, Danny Mowl drums.

Q. Who are your influences?

A. We've actually been playing together for about six years, so we no longer try to be like anyone but of the modern bands we like GuanaBatz, Restless and Batmobile.

Q. Have any of you played with previous bands?

A. We were previously known as Shakeout and before that Spellbound.

Q. What involvement has Boz Boorer with the band?

A. I've known Boz since he was with The Polecats and he has produced our records and got us the early breaks in London.

Q. Who does most of the songwriting?

A. Ian and myself write most songs and Boz as you probably know wrote High Class Power (Klub Foot Three) and has written a number of songs for us which we may put in the set later in the year.

Q. How did you get the name Wigsvile Spliffs?

A. Wigsville is an imaginery place name on the back of an old record of Rock 'N' Roll music from America and Spliff was a slang term in the U.S.A. before it it became a slang word over here for a drug (smoke).

Q. Have you toured abroad?

A. Yes, we played a festival in France and are due to go to Germany to gig with Batmobile soon and so some work on our own. Later in the year we are going to Belgium, Holland, Germany, France, Switzerland and Austria.

Q. What plans have The Spliffs for the future?

A. We are about to record an album in a few months' time with Boz and we hope to have it out by the end of the year.

Mike also told me during one of our phone calls that the Song Al Capone was written due to his interest in American gangsters. Top bloke, top band sadly overlooked.

The Go-Katz.

Howard Piperides owned Raucous Records which was a Psychobilly/Rockabilly mail order company and a newly formed record label. I bought many a record from him which the local record shops could not get hold of. He was also the vocalist in The Go-Katz an emerging band from the scene around Loughborough. He agreed to provide a mostly self-written piece about his band:

A band you may not have heard of yet - The Go-Katz but having just released their first 4 track E.P. and playing on the bill at the Belgium Psycho Festival alongside such bands as Frenzy, Demented Are Go, Torment, Long Tall Texans etc. It looks like you could hear a lot more from them in the future. The band can be found around Loughborough, Leicester and consist of:

Wolf, drums. Digs early Restless, Rapids etc. Also likes the odd bit of Reggae. Was very upset when his blow-up doll was unfaithful at a party. The doll then got ripped to pieces and Wolf has never been the same.

Andy, lead guitar. Likes early Punk and Modern Rockabilly (GuanaBatz etc) writes most Go-Katz songs including three of the four on The Go-Katz e.p.. Previous bands include Captain Scarlett and The Mysterons and The Go-Go Dakotas.

Beaker, rhythm guitar. Into sex, ciggies and The Meteors. Writes one song every two years. His latest effort is 'Beaker Boogie' which is an instrumental dedicated to Lisa Hurst who was stabbed to death by her boyfriend after he had been listening to The Meteors. Founder member of The Excorcists.

Moff, slap bass. Likes trad 50's Rockabilly and also digs The Sting-Rays. Smokes cigars, gets bevvied! Formerly slapped for The Go-Go Dakotas.

H.P. vocals. Responsible for writing 'Brain Decay'. Owner of oversized quiff! Likes most Psychobilly including The Meteors, Archie etc, Trash including The Sting-Rays, The Vibes, TallBoys and Rockabilly including Stray Cats, Deltas and Gene Vincent.

The Go-Katz were formed in September 1986 from the wreckage of The Exorcists and The Go-Go Dakotas. A month after their formation they supported Torment and The Blubbery Hellbellies and recorded a 5-track demo of which the legendary Go-Katz track 'Brain Decay' came. The Go-Katz also headlined a 4-band line up at Loughborough University of which the band say was "our worst performance so far" but the local press didn't agree as in December the band were featured in their local newspapers. 1987 has been just as hectic for the band playing alongside The Coffin Nails and at a scooterists do and as I mentioned at the first Psycho Festival in Belgium. The Go-Katz have also just released their first dynamic 4 track e.p. which was recorded in March and features Nightmares as the main track and the other tracks are Fine Thing Baby, Nowhere Train and No Gene Vincent.

The Pharaohs.

The Pharaohs were a Nervous Records band hailing from Harlow, Essex. They were featured on Stomping at The Klub Foot Volume Two and sounded fresh, powerful and exciting. The sound that was captured on the Klub Foot album never managed to be reproduced on any of their subsequent releases. They had released an l.p. Blue Egypt on Nervous which in my opinion was hampered by the production, although the band sounded tight the potential of a classic was lost. In the following interview I very briefly touched on the subject. I always thought the song writing was strong which was proven by songs such as Blue Egypt, Keep on Running and Dead to The World. The Pharaohs were only featured in issue one, even though I remember speaking to affable singer Glenn Daeche on the telephone, no further interviews were planned. I think the reason was partly due to wanting to feature and contact as many bands as I could and there wasn't enough time to revisit all the bands.

Drummer of the band Nick Becker answered my questions, after I had obtained his address from a Nervous Records release.

The Pharaohs have led a pretty quiet existence during the last few months. With the release of their Vigilante 12"on Nervous Records things seem to be picking up again for the band. Having previously released an album on Nervous, Blue Egypt and also being featured on compilation albums such as Zorch Factor One, Stomping at The Klub Foot Volume Two etc, The Pharaohs have built up a healthy following throughout Europe.

Here drummer of the band Nick Becker answers my questions about the band.

Q. When were The Pharaohs formed?

A. January 1985.

Q. What were the band members doing before they formed the band?

A. Nick Becker (me), drums - playing for various Pop bands in Harlow, Lee Brown, bass - playing for a Psychobilly band called Trash, Ben Evans, guitar - playing for a Punk band called The Spelling Mistakes. Glen Daeche, vocals, guitar - has been playing for only The Pharaohs and has had a band called The Pharaohs since 1981.

Q. Who are The Pharaohs main influences?

A. Their mums and dads. We don't have any influences as a band but of course have our own favourite musicians.

Q. What happened to Jeff Horsey your old bassist?

A. Jeff had enough of touring and not getting pots of money. He is now a window dresser for a manikin manufacturer.

Q. How much of a boost to your careers was it by appearing on the Klub Foot l.p.?

A. The Klub Foot l.p. was really the key to us playing throughout Europe.

Q. How well have The Pharaohs done abroad?

A. The Pharaohs are very big in Germany not so big in Holland.

Q. How did you get the record deal with Nervous?

A. Nervous were negotiating a deal before the Klub Foot l.p. They had seen us downstairs at The Clarendon.

Q. Were you happy with the Blue Egypt l.p.?

A. We weren't entirely happy with Blue Egypt although we feel it was an acceptable first try.

Q. I read that you thought Rockabilly/Rock 'N'Roll was being wasted by traditionalists who wasted the music by keeping it stuck in the fifties, do you think that The Pharaohs and the new breed of Rockin' bands have helped stamp this traditionalism out?

A. We don't not like traditional Rockabilly we just don't try to put it into our music. We wouldn't like to completely get rid of it. It is mainly the ignorant few Teds that won't accept the new breed of music we would like to stamp these out.

A while after this interview was published, I was working for a Plumbers merchant and was sent on a customer service course in Harlow, Essex. I remember staring out of the window of the classroom and seeing Nick Becker (or someone who strongly resembled him) walking past. Small world.

Long Tall Texans.

The Long Tall Texans hailing from Brighton, a very polished, tight, and well-rehearsed band, have gained a huge reputation within the scene. Always a very popular live act with singer and bass slapper Mark Carew's permanent cheery demeanour. At the time of the article the band had just released their well-produced 'Sodbusters' album, after appearing on quite a few compilation albums. They were radio friendly whilst also maintaining that slight edge. I imagine if they had been pushed more aggressively, they could have achieved some form of mainstream success. The track 'Non-Stop Loving' which was featured on the Nervous Records compilation 'Zorch Factor One' was at the time one of my favourite songs. I decided that they had to have a feature in issue one. Mark Denman the bands guitarist and by profession a teacher was my contact within the band, and he kindly sent me the Long Tall Texans contribution.

The Long Tall Texans are: -

Mark Carew, slap bass, vocals.

Mark Denman, guitar.

Theo, drums.

"The Texans have been together now for 3 years. They were formed by the two Marks after the split of Brighton Rockabilly band 'The Asteroids'. Since then, the band has been gigging constantly around the South of England and London, building up a solid following but it is only over the last year with the release of the tracks on 'Zorch Factor One' and 'The Rockin' Won't Stop' albums that The Texans have achieved wider acclaim. Since then, The Long Tall Texans have received fan mail from all over Britain and Europe. Playing alongside bands like The Meteors, GuanaBatz, Restless and Frenzy at venues like The Klub Foot and 100 Club. Punters now realise that The Texans are a serious band to be reckoned with. Frenzy are good friends of ours and doing 20 gigs in a month, covering 4500 miles around Europe all living in their C-reg coach was an epic experience. Hopefully there will be more of that to come for us. The Long Tall Texans first l.p. is now out it's called 'Sodbusters' and it's on Razor Records, RAZ 23. After two weeks the initial pressing of 2000 copies had sold out and more are being made to deal with the demand. We've signed for three l.p.'s so the past years of hard slogging have paid off at last." The Long Tall Texans have also just recorded a 4 track E.P. which includes a remixed version of album track 'Poison' plus three new tracks, so watch out for that. Just one more thing Mark, tell us about Mark Carew's crazy slap bass playing technique. "Mark's suicidal bass slapping technique originates from a childhood habit of stealing hubcaps from moving cars. Most bass players have to tape up their fingers when playing The Long Tall Texans have to tape up their bass!"

During a phone call to Mark, he suggested that I should include a news section in The Crazed, I never took this suggestion on board as I assumed that the news would be out of date by the time the zine was released, and I certainly didn't run by any deadlines.

Torment.

Torment emerged with their own look and sound, merging Rockabilly, Psychobilly and Punk. Singer and guitarist Simon Brand had previously been in Frenzy but jumped ship before Frenzy's popularity built. The band had become a popular feature at the Klub Foot and also appeared on Stomping at The Klub Foot Volume Three as well as the video accompanying the album. They had released their debut album Psyclops Carnival and a 12" e.p. Mystery Men on Nervous Records. I recently checked on the internet and Psyclops Carnival will now set you back about £30.00. Although the band played Psychobilly, they were not comparable to any other band at the time. Torment were a band helping to push Psychobilly forward and were unique. I regret not having a face-to-face interview with the band, although I'm pretty pleased with the features in issues one and three. Kevin Haynes the bands drummer was a top bloke and really helped me with The Crazed as you will find out later in the book. He kindly answered my questions I sent him. Here is the interview along with my wacky see how many Torment songs I can feature in the introduction.

It was a NIGHTMARE at the PSYCLOPS CARNIVAL, what with UNCLE SAM telling us about the CON-SCRIPTION PLAN on how to join the DEATH TRAIL to find the MYSTERY MAN who committed the RED DEATH. What a HEAD DRIVEN SINNER he is. Some people reckon it was THE LAST TIME he'll do it, whilst others with TIME TO THINK reckon he might SLOW DOWN, but I reckon that you should get to THE SOURCE of it. But look up in the sky at the ROCKJET it's Simon Brand, Simon Crowfoot and Kevin Haynes who appear to the public under the guise of TORMENT. Maybe they can help UNCLE SAM out?

With singer and guitarist Simon Brand previously playing for Frenzy and Simon Crowfoot previously slapping his bass for those rubber luvvas Demented Are Go it seems like these are the right people to hunt the MYSTERY MAN down. But what experience have they had? Well they've released an an L.P. called PSYCLOPS CARNIVAL on

Nervous as well as the MYSTERY MEN 12" e.p. They've also appeared on various compilation l.p.'s including Stomping at The Klub Foot Volume Three, Psycho Attack Over Europe Volume Two etc. They've even appeared on the Klub Foot video, and they can also be found regularly inhabiting the stage at the Klub Foot. Also not forgetting that they're recording a new l.p. for Nervous soon. UNCLE SAM is impressed. Drummer of the band Kevin Haynes agreed to disclose some information on Torment. He sits down while we focus the spotlight on him.

Q. Who was in the original Torment line up?

A. I (Kev) started Torment with our old bassist Sean Holder who wrote Death Trail but musically he got left behind, so myself and Si (Brand) got Tony Biggs who was with The Firebirds at the time. Things didn't work out with him either so entered Simon Crowfoot, the present line up. The new Torment had begun.

Q. What is Uncle Sam about?

A. Uncle Sam was conceived in about five minutes in a small practice studio in Bristol about nineteen months ago. It's a war song with humour! Maybe it's about the hot-headed American GI's it's crazy.

Q. Why did Simon Brand leave Frenzy?

A. Simon Brand and Steve Whitehouse are both personalities in their own right. You can never have two leaders in one band it just don't work. I think that's the reason but who knows the truth? In Torment we all have our own duties to do within the band, so arguments are rare!

Q. How did you get the deal with Nervous?

A. I sent a dodgy demo to Nervous they saw it had promise so they got on the phone to me the day after and said they were interested but get a gig in London! which is harder than it sounds! We started recording two weeks after our first Klub Foot.

Q. Who are your inspirations?

A. Simon Brands are Punk, Sex Pistols, Demented and Johnny Rotten. Simon Crowfoot likes all the old classics Joe Clay, Johnny Burnette. Kev's (mine) Nutty Dave, Johnny Burnette/ Hasil Adkins.

Q. Were you happy with the songs chosen for the Klub Foot l.p.?

A. We chose the songs ourselves; we were surprised we had three songs along with Batmobile. I think the Klub Foot album have shown Torment are a live band and not just a band who make great records!

Q. Were you happy with the way you came over on the Klub Foot video?

A. The video was good considering the lighting wasn't very good and the sound was taken straight off the video microphones. But I think we all came across quite well.

Q. What have Torment got planned for the future?

A. To make lots of money so we can give our jobs up and concentrate on the music. More tours are being lined up and it would be nice to be signed up by a nice major record company with money to promote Torment and Psychobilly.

Alas the money and major record company never came but Kevin's comments about Torment's future plans brought back a little of the eighties optimism which seems refreshing now compared to some of the hopelessness around presently. Kevin was always open to discussing the scene and Torment during my phone calls and once mistook an information gathering call for an interview, "I thought this was an interview" he disappointedly said. Simon Brand is sadly no longer with us and is very much missed by all who followed Torment and Psychobilly.

Compiling issue 1.

So that was that content for issue one. The next job was to compile all the material together and create a (hopefully) readable fanzine. I borrowed my Mum's typewriter and set upon the long task of transcribing everything, my drive and excitement got me through it all. The idea that my work could morph into a fanzine that I hoped somebody would want to buy and read was a strong motivator to get it finished. I soon realised that due to the short length of most of the interviews the pages would look rather sparse, more blank space than text. A black felt tip pen solved this problem by allowing me to add funky borders and other basic designs. A pair of scissors were also acquired to add images that were included on numerous flyers I had received from the bands. I also included an advert from Nervous Records for Torment's Mystery Men e.p. which I took from one of the music papers, free advertising! not great business acumen! I contacted Howard Piperides vocalist for the Go-Katz to help with the distribution of The Crazed and be a contact address. He had started a Psychobilly/Rockabilly mail order business called Raucous Records selling many of the harder to find releases. This was probably not my greatest idea as I had no control of any correspondence that the fanzine received and released a little control away from me. I gave Raucous Records a free half page advert for their assistance. A cover and an introduction were also needed. What could go on the cover? another ropey sketch of a mutant similar to the one I sent 54321 fanzine? I decided against that and came up with a not so truly original idea, I copied a sketch of a double bass from a Nervous Records flyer. Not exactly the most eye catching but this predicament would resolve itself for future issues. For the introduction I cobbled together the following (edited version):

Hallo, good evening and welcome, well here it is the very first issue of The Crazed. What can I say? except that I hope you like it and buy future issues because I want to become rich and famous. As you can see The Crazed features interviews, articles on modern rockin' bands, although I like the old stuff, I don't think it's worth dwelling in the past that much when there is so much fresh talent around today in the rockin' scene (even though the music press can't see it). Apart from the address and merchandising Raucous Records has no other connection with The Crazed. Well, that's about it. Hope you enjoy The Crazed and look out for issue two. Cheers, Paul W

Printing issue 1.

The final step was to get the finished product printed. A new printing shop had opened in the high street and looked in my inexperienced view a perfect place to use. So, into the shop I went with an envelope of A4 size completed pages of The Crazed ready to print. I remember a member of staff being decked out in shirt and tie taking me seriously, a teenage Psychobilly with pages of obscure (to them) bands. I asked for them to print/photocopy the fanzine and make it A5 size as I thought it would look better and more compact instead of A4 size. I can't remember the price or the amount but was told to return later in the week to collect the finished product. My anticipation and excitement were high when I went to collect the printed copies. The staff smiled and showed me a large box on the floor which seemed a bit odd for an A5 sized fanzine. They then proudly showed me the first printed copy, I couldn't believe they had printed it A4 size, not what I had asked for. It didn't look great. I left the printers speechless with a much heavier than expected box under my arm. I never used the shop again and it later closed. So, off the copies went to be sold. I produced a small flyer that I sent to Roy Williams of Nervous Records to include in his next mail out of his informative Zorch News, it included a speech bubble from a Psychobilly I had drawn saying "Exposure at last!". The fanzine was 40p plus 20p postage and packing or 40p overseas. The Crazed seemed to be selling fairly well and I started receiving a bit of correspondence from readers. I have included a few examples (not always complimentary).

'Just writing to congratulate you on a brilliant mag!!! I wondered whether it would be a good idea to do an article on Frenzy? Also, I have just finished a 2-year graphics and design course and am a pretty good artist. I would love to do something for your mag? Can't wait for issue 2 of The Crazed (should be spelt with a K!!).'

'At last a Psycho mag that's going to get somewhere. I hope you don't mind but I took the liberty of sending you a review of the

Batmobile gig at the Klub Foot on July 25th. I thought you might like to use it in a future edition of The Crazed (it was used in issue 2 and will be included in a later chapter). Oh yes, I also gave Ant Thomas of Demented a fag once. Also, if you're in London without a bed for the nite - don't hesitate to call us.'

'Well done Crazed it just shows that someone has more sense than the music press, keep up the good work. We write to bands but we get no replies don't get me wrong travelling to England is great but we just can't afford it. So how about coming to Scotland for once.'

'I would like to congratulate you on having the initiative to tap an as yet unrecognised market. It's good to see that there is someone with the ability to go where no music press has gone and actually pay service to Psychobilly/Rockabilly music. However, despite the novelty and excitement of actually reading about bands I like instead of what Boy George does in his spare time. I feel that the magazine needs a bit of improving. I have a few interesting ideas but I don't think I'll tell you them because I was going to start up a fanzine but maybe there's no point now. Maybe you could consider taking me on as a writer or something seeing that you are taking away my business. I have had a little experience at writing articles for magazines.' (no examples were provided).

'I am glad to see a magazine aimed at this particular music which is commonly exploited by the music press who are more interested in bands like The Communards. I think The Crazed is an excellent mag but could do with more live reviews. Coming from the North East I don't get to see many bands as hardly any travel up here.'

I was also sent drawings similar to what I had done with 54321 from people hoping to get their designs on the cover. The Crazed seemed to be reaching out to people like me. This was not the age of the internet where one click can connect you to hundreds of others with the same interest, everything was all mostly down to word of mouth.

During this rather hectic time I went to see GuanaBatz for the first time at the Angel Centre in Tonbridge. One of the Psychobilly's I went up there with seemed to panic when he entered the venue at the sight of other Psychobilly's with their DM's and carelessly swigging lager or whatever cheap slop was on sale. I thought it was funny as he was dressed and looked the same. I do remember some of the crazier Psychobilly's pulling themselves up on ropes to the ceiling of the venue (it must have also been used as a gym) and sitting on a ledge close to the top whilst their quiffs got flattened by the ceiling, looking back one fall could have broken a lot of bones or possibly killed someone! What a few pints can make you do! The bouncers soon called them down. When the Batz came on I distinctly remember the first member was Diddle who sat behind his drums. The records that I had played constantly in my room were now being performed live right in front of a room of like-minded people. It felt magical!

Issue 2.

I had already started working on issue 2 before the release of issue 1, my enthusiasm knew no bounds. I did not want another issue full of interviews conducted by questions and answers received through the post. I wanted to undertake face to face interviews to actually meet the bands and become known on the scene. Issue 1 was okay, but that format could not be sustained as my readership would get bored and to be honest anyone could send questions to the bands themselves. Face to face interviews would give The Crazed more credibility. Also, in a selfish way I wanted to meet the bands and get to know them. I was now able to ring the bands and attempt to arrange interviews often speaking to their managers who knew that I was genuine as The Crazed had been released and I was not some deranged fan trying to meet their idols.

The Meteors.

I had found out that a rockin' band from Tunbridge Wells called Fractured who were starting to become Klub Foot regulars, were playing at the Angel Centre in Tonbridge on 02nd May 1987 supporting The Meteors. I went to the nearest public phone box armed with numerous 10p pieces and contacted the band and arranged an interview with them to be conducted before the gig. It always amuses me how confident I was ringing all these bands and arranging interviews or gathering information, I don't ever recall being nervous or hesitant, I presume the teenage me had a goal and that was to feature as many of my favourite bands in The Crazed.

I now had to compile a list of questions, buy a cassette for my trusty tape recorder, and head off to the sunny climes of Tonbridge. Being a record fanatic as soon as I got off the train, I searched for the nearest record shop and with a vinyl hunting instinct found one. I automatically went straight to the Rockabilly/Rock 'N' Roll section and started searching and found the compilation album 'James Deans of The Dole Queue' which featured a track from Fractured. So, with tape recorder in one hand and newly bought album in the other I set off on my quest to the Angel Centre. Upon entering the Centre, I approached the receptionist and showed her a card I had printed stating Paul W editor of The Crazed, (pretty flash uh?) she smiled and pointed to a door and told me that the bands were rehearsing inside. After thanking her I walked over and opened the door and saw only one person on the stage, I could not believe it, the one person who for me summed up Psychobilly, leader of my favourite band and Psychobilly God...P. Paul Fenech! I could not let this moment pass, so right from the back of the hall I loudly yelled out "Hello, I'm Paul Wainwright I run a fanzine called The Crazed is it possible to do an interview?" He looked slightly impressed when I mentioned that the fanzine was called The Crazed and agreed to the interview, inviting me up on stage with him whilst he was tuning his guitar. This was more than anything I could have ever imagined, an interview with

The Meteors. They had been interviewed by the music press even making the front page of Sounds and been featured on the Radio 1 John Peel show and they were now being interviewed by me for my first face to face interview. So, with very wobbly legs I made my way to the stage.

Fortunately, in the very distant hope that The Meteors would agree to be interviewed I had a list of questions already prepared in my pocket. Nervously I pressed the record button on my tape recorder and with shaking hands unfolded the questions. I seemed to have gained a very dodgy fake cockney accent, but here I was standing next to P. Paul Fenech. I remember looking at the tattoos on his arm that were within inches of me. He continued tuning his guitar with various roadies and band members walking around whilst answering my questions. Here is the interview as it appeared in issue 2.

The first true Psychobilly band The Meteors. The band that first started mixing traditional Rockabilly with a heavier more aggressive sound and also writing their lyrics in a horror B-movie style. While everybody else was singing about cruising around in their Cadillacs The Meteors sang songs about Werewolves, Earwigs and of course Rockabilly Psychosis. So, when Nigel Lewis first picked up his double bass, P. Paul Fenech plugged his guitar in and Mark Robertson picked up his drum sticks did they know at that time they would change the style of modern Rockabilly in this country. They mixed the traditional sound with the energy and enthusiasm of Punk which was still a strong influence on many bands around the time The Meteors were formed. Whereas there was a slight Rockabilly movement in the national charts during the early eighties, which was led by The Stray Cats and followed by bands such as The Polecats (which featured Boz Boorer) etc. The Meteors although signed to a major label Island Records didn't quite fit into the same mould as these bands and weren't pushed enough to become a chart band. Although this may have been fortunate for the band as other bands around that time have all either split up or sunk into oblivion (excepting maybe The Jets). The Meteors have kept their solid loyal following all the time and have also been the original inspiration behind most of (if not all) the Psychobilly bands that have followed in their wake.

Although there have been many different line-up changes, P.Paul Fenech being the only original band member left, he has always managed to keep The Meteors sound intact and always keeping to their original ideals. I asked P.Paul Fenech and his band some questions about The Meteors.

I wondered what the band though of all these records such as 'Curse Of The Mutants' and the 'Wreckin'Crew' 12" e.p. (to name a couple) which include all previously released songs, P. Paul explains: "I think it's just a rip off really 'cos it ain't nothing to do with The Meteors now days, it's just putting records in different packages to get money out of people for nothing basically". But due to the strength of The Meteors reputation all the records chart in the indie charts. The Meteors have also moved from Mad Pig Records to Anagram Records (who had previously had bands such as Sunglasses After Dark, Alien Sex Fiend etc) P. Paul explains why they changed labels: "Mad Pig's my own record label so I just use that for other bands, but Anagram's got more money than I have". So, you'll still use Mad Pig yourself? "I'll use it for some stuff, but I won't be doing no more Meteors stuff on it". Signing up new bands? "If I can find some good ones yeah".

As I wrote earlier The Meteors have got through many line ups, why does P. Paul get through so many band members? "Because I'm a bastard trying to find some other bastards to work with me but now, I've found a couple of real bastards". Toby Griffin (who used to drum for The Coffin Nails) replaced Ian 'Spider' Cubitt on drums. I asked Toby how he came to join The Meteors: "The Meteors asked me as they had a bit of trouble with the last drummer. He left to get married the day before they went to Germany and they phoned a promoter in London who does the Klub Foot and asked him for any Psychobilly drummers and he gave them my phone number, and they phoned me up and said have you got a whole week spare starting from tomorrow 'cos we're going to Germany and could you stand in for us, so I said yeah. We were going to sound check when we got there in Munich, but we had so much trouble getting there that we got there half an hour before we got on stage. So, I'd been listening to all the stuff on a Walkman and we just went on and played. They hadn't heard me and I hadn't played with them before or anything and they asked me to stay so I did".

In The Meteors original line up P. Paul and Nigel Lewis used to split the songs between them with each of them singing and writing their own songs. This shows on the band's records at the time when the records were half P. Paul's and half Nigel's. Some of Nigel's songs were classic Meteors Psychobilly such as Radioactive Kid, Rockabilly Psychosis etc. When he left The Meteors, Nigel formed a Garage Punk band called The Escalators and he swapped the double bass for an electric bass. After The Escalators he formed The Tall Boys and now he's recording solo albums for Media Burn Records, the first of which was recorded in his bedroom in Pimlico, London. I asked P. Paul what he thought of the stuff Nigel is doing now: "I haven't heard none of it, but I know he's a good bloke". Why did he split from the band a while back? "'Cos, he wanted to do sort of Psychedelic stuff and I didn't want to do it". Clapham South Escalators sort of stuff? "Yeah, I didn't want to do it really". The Clapham South Escalators e.p. was a record which The Meteors recorded under a pseudonym during the end of the recording of their debut 'In Heaven' album, it featured the band playing in a more sixties influenced Garage sound. I asked P. Paul what he thought of the record: "It was alright we only did it for a laugh, but he wanted to take it seriously". After Nigel Lewis left the band, they have gone through a succession of electric bass players, would The Meteors ever revert back to a double bass? "No, its old fashioned". Since The Meteors appeared with their original brand of Psychobilly, they've influenced many bands to imitate their style. I wondered what P.Paul thought of these bands: "I hate them all, I hate every single one of them. I hate every single band apart from The Meteors and that's the God's honest truth". A track on the Sewertime Blues album 'Mind Over Matter' seems to take this point up, I asked P.Paul about the song: "That's slagging off everybody King Kurt what's the other lot? GuanaBatz and anybody who thinks their doing something different when they're not".

During their many gigs The Meteors have had a few brushes with the law, one gig that I particularly remember was one reported in Sounds a while back in which P.Paul had to appear in court about (I remember something about cymbals being used as frisbees): "Which one was that?" P. Paul says jokingly: "My tour manager got out of hand. No, it was just like a bunch of yobs causing trouble, so we removed them from the hall sort of thing". Do you ever regret getting the violent following you attract sometimes? "I'm not violent and I don't think I've got a violent image what they do is up to them really. I play violent music though".

The Meteors have recently filmed one of their gigs which will probably be released as a follow up to their 'Live at The Hellfire Club' video which was released on Jettisoundz. What did P.Paul think of that original video? "I think it's a bit limp really. It's alright 'cos it's The Meteors but it's not a good interpretation of a good Meteors gig". Talking of live recordings, I wondered whether 'The Meteors Live Volume Two' was an official Meteors release as it was released on Dojo who had previously released 'The Curse of The Mutants' album which The Meteors wished to disassociate themselves from. P. Paul explains: "Yes that was one of mine'" But it was on Dojo? "Some of it is some of it ain't, the second pressing is on Dojo and the first ones on Anagram I think". Anagram have recently released The Meteors sixth studio album 'Don't Touch the Bang Bang Fruit' which at the time of this interview was secret Meteors information.

Talking earlier of videos I believe that P.Paul has got an extensive video collection, P.Paul explains: "Well it's more my Dad's now 'cos I moved out and he's got four hundred and eighty and they're mainly horror films anything violent". That's where you get a lot of your influences from? "Yeah, I watch a lot of tele". So apart from the films who influences your song writing? "I do, it all comes from me and the band it don't come from nobody else". The Meteors last few singles have all been cover versions songs such as Jan and Deans 'Surf City', The Stranglers 'Go Buddy Go' to name a couple. I wondered why they release so many cover versions as singles on which P. Paul simply answers: "I like the songs". So out of all the records he's released what's been his favourite? "The next one" he jokes.

What an achievement an interview with undoubtably the biggest band on the scene and also my favourite band. It might not have been an in-depth interview but for me The Crazed had reached a high point. The fanzine was named after a Meteors song and now the fanzine was to feature an interview with The Meteors. I could have stopped then and have felt that it was all worth it, but I was still on a mission to feature more bands that I liked. I remember later talking to a Psychobilly from Reading outside the Klub Foot about The Crazed and he could not believe that I had interviewed The Meteors "No it wasn't you" he said. "Yes, it was" I proudly replied to his disbelieving face.

Fractured.

Fractured who I had originally arranged the interview at the Angel Centre with entered the hall and looked disapprovingly at me on stage interviewing The Meteors "You are here to interview us" lead singer Paul Everdell hollered as soon as he saw me. I wasn't bothered their questions were in my pocket and there was enough room on the tape for another interview.

Fractured were a popular band at the Klub Foot and the band's name often got hollered out during other bands sets. There is one recording of the Guanabatz at the Klub Foot during which a member of the audience can be heard yelling 'Fractured'. They were a very tight neo-Rockabilly band and could not be described as Psychobilly even though their music was appreciated by a Psychobilly audience due to the speed and excitement of the bands playing. They also did an excellent cover of Jimmy Dean's 'Big Bad John' which would certainly get a wrecking pit going. To conduct the interview, we found an empty room and as I sat on the floor surrounded by the band, I got my list of questions out of my pocket and pressed the red record button on the cassette recorder. I also asked them to write down their favourite top ten records, the results just made it into issue 1. Here is my second face to face interview.

A relatively new band on the scene Fractured although they have been formed for nearly two years, but it's been worth them waiting as they've become a popular band at the Klub Foot and have also been featured on Northwood/ID's rockin' compilation album 'James Deans of the Dole Queue' and there are also plans for a possible album in the future. The band come from Tunbridge Wells and have built up a healthy following in and around their hometown, a lot of whom they bring to their gigs with them in organised coaches. I found the band about to go on stage in Tonbridge (right next to Tunbridge Wells) and the first rather obvious question I asked them was how did the band get together? singer and guitarist Paul Everdell answers: "I played with the drummer (Squit) who's the best about and then met Nick one night at a Restless gig 'cos we didn't know who he was and found out he only lived a little way down the road and played bass. We started playing after eighteen months, we decided we were a bit to hollow and we couldn't get what we wanted out of a three piece, so we advertised and the next thing Mr Herman came knocking on the door". Mr Herman being Mike Herman who joined the band on rhythm guitar.

So, with the history of the band sorted out I asked them what stands Fractured apart from other rockin' bands, Paul: "If we say something like they're all as good as we are people are going to say we're modest and if we say musically, we're better, our songs make sense, they're going to say what a big-headed bunch of bastards. I think we have got a different style and I think the songs make sense". Playing at the Klub Foot seemed to be the push that Fractured needed to become a popular band on the rockin' circuit. The band believe it's been harder for them to get themselves known as: "We're out in the sticks we're not near the action" as Paul explains. But the band are confident about their future as Paul continues: "From what I can see at the moment, the following we've got is growing in a relatively short space of time and the people who come to see us like it. If people now like it, then surely there's more who will like it when they hear us. We like it ourselves and I think you've got to like what you're playing". Liking their music is something the band agree in, as Paul describes his band: "I listened to a demo we'd done up the Klub Foot the other week and I don't think listening to it that you wouldn't hear a better interpretation of modern Rockabilly music. I feel if I wasn't writing it and I went up to see the band I'd like it. I think it was good the drumming wasn't too heavy it's heavier than authentic but not Psycho".

Although the band are impressed by their demos they weren't over impressed by their track 'Dark Blue Sea' on the 'James Deans of The Dole Queue' compilation album, as Paul explains: "If we'd been there when it was engineered, we'd have wanted a different sound to that, that is not us. The only reason we were on it is because Boz Boorer liked the track when we recorded it and he just at the time said he'd put it down, but to how we play it now a year on we play it so much better anyway. But if we was to record it now, I think it would be fifty times better as we would play it faster and more aggressively, for a start put a bit of energy into it".

Fractured have played a couple of concerts which have been billed as 'Psychobilly Nights' something which the band are not too happy about as Paul explains: "We're not Psychobilly we're modern Rockabilly. I don't think we do any number that you could classify as Psychobilly. We don't want to play Psychobilly it's too heavy". Some people have compared Fractured with Restless something of which the band wish to make clear: "We're probably as far away as what Restless play as Gary Glitter or something like that, miles away. We've listened to a lot of Restless, we like Restless. I think Mark Harman is a very good guitarist, but I don't think we're influenced by them to that extent. I think we play slightly heavier music than they do or did" explained Paul.

As Fractured are a modern Rockabilly band what do they think of bands who keep their music stuck in the fifties? Nick Hoadley the bands bassist answers: "Some of them are really good, they keep going round in circles, none of them are going to get anywhere but a lot of them are really good. They're good musicians". On a lighter note, I ask the band what has been their worst gig, Nick immediately answers: "The Clay Pidgeon supporting The Hayriders where we blew the bass amp up". Paul: "The bass amp blew up before we even started". Nick: "At the soundcheck". Paul: "We was a three piece then which the bass didn't help and we didn't go down with an authentic crowd".

Paul then explains where he would like to see Fractured in the future: "We want to be big in Europe, play in this country with people saying they're good musicians. Like I'm not going to see them 'cos they swear on stage and instigate a bit of violence. I want to go and see them because they play good music and they're entertaining to watch". Mike: " I want to get recognised in the street by fourteen-year-olds!". So, what have Fractured got planned for the future? Paul: "More women, you just write in your magazine that I'm single". Mike: "I'm very single, so single there's only half of me". Paul: "And you can stick our addresses and numbers down". Mike: "And put a photo of Nick Kamen next to my name!". Paul: "And they've got to send a photo.... naked!". "We'd like to think we're going somewhere. I think we will if we stick to it, I don't think there's anything that will stop us". Mike: "Except your socks which you've been wearing for the last century I've noticed".

I took a couple of photos of the band with my Kodak Disc Camera (remember those), unfortunately they were too dark to print in the fanzine. Instead, I included some dodgy portraits I drew of each member. When I later saw singer Paul at a gig, I asked for his opinion, did he like them "Not really" he honestly replied. I later met Boz Boorer who told me that he was not too impressed regarding the band's comments about the production of 'Dark Blue Sea'. I also saw one of Fractured (name withheld) at the Klub Foot who was not having a pleasant evening due to rival bands followers, I think he was on his own as once he saw me, he came straight over and started chatting, such was the rivalry between bands. Fractured later released a mini album 'No Rest for The Wicked' on ID Records which featured a cracking version of 'Big Bad John'.

Dendermonde Psycho Festival
1987 review.

Howard Piperides from Raucous Records sent me a review of the 1987 Psycho Festival held between 18th and 19th of April in Dendermonde, Belgium. His band The Go-Katz were also on the bill and surprisingly received a less than flattering write up. His review was a lot more critical than my favourable record reviews featured in issue one which I had decided to stop so that I had more space to interview more bands. This decision unfortunately stopped me from receiving any free records, although Roy Williams did send me a copy of Torment's Three a Crowd album which sticking to my policy I never reviewed, he never sent me anymore! So, in all its glory here is the review as it appeared in issue two:

On a no expense spared trip The Crazed sent roving reporter Howard Piperides out to Belgium during April to review the Psycho Festival that was being held there. But it happened to be that H.P. was actually in one of the bands on the bill at the festival, The Go-Katz and he had already paid for his trip (ok, so we knew all the time he was going and we weren't really going to pay his trip). So now read the on-spot review of the festival by someone that was not only there to watch it but also performed on stage. Take it away H.P.......

With the 'Psycho Festival' not beginning until 8.00pm most of Saturday was spent in the Dendermonde marketplace. The locals didn't know quite what had hit them as hundreds of Psychobilly's lined the streets drinking and sleeping in the sun. Despite being closely watched by the police waiting for a riot to begin, spirits were good with everyone piling on top of each other for a wild photo session!

In the evening what was billed as a 'Psychobilly Party' took place. It was actually a disco and video show which featured 'Blood on the Cats', 'Stomping at the Klub Foot', The Meteors and the GuanaBatz on film with the disco spinning a good selection of Psychobilly, Rockabilly and Trash.

Sunday was devoted to the seven bands appearing at the festival, kicking off with local boys The Ratmen a four piece with the double bassist and the drummer standing out as outstanding musicians. Although what they played was run of the mill Psychobilly with nothing too daring or complicated, they were obviously very well-rehearsed. Their set was a mixture of self-penned songs and covers with a few instrumentals thrown in for good measure. They may not be the most musically adventurous band but if safe Psychobilly is your thing The Ratmen are well worth seeing.

Second on the bill were my own Quiffabilly quintet The Go-Katz who were definitely the sexiest band to play. The attempt at the debut single 'Nightmare' was a complete mess but that can mainly be blamed on alcohol abuse. Things never really got back together again until near the end of the set with 'Real Gone Demented Hillbilly Cat' and 'Fine Thing Baby' being the best songs.

Nervous Records main man Roy Williams introduced Torment, the Mystery Men. They received a well-deserved tremendous reception from the crowd throughout their faultless performance. They played their tracks from the 'Zorch Factor One' compilation along with most of the songs from their 'Psyclops Carnival' album, an album which is not really a true representation of an essentially live band. The songs which stood out as best were 'Rock Strong' and 'Mystery Man' from their latest 12".

The best reception went to Batmobile maybe because for the Europeans they typify what Psychobilly is all about. But to your average 'Britabilly' I imagine that dressing up as Cavemen and playing songs like 'Scum of the Neighbourhood', 'Bat Attack' and 'Transylvanian Express' might seem a little corny. To give them credit though they were the most professional and polished band to play whilst at the same time keeping the raw edge that makes Psychobilly what it is.

The subject of rough raw edge brings us nicely to Demented Are Go who are basically nothing but rough raw edge! To put it plainly

Demented Are Go were a complete shambles! Maybe it was too much to expect that vocalist Mark Phillips much the worst for alcohol would remember his lyrics and stay vertical he did neither! The trio plus their combusting washboard player were tonight re-joined by ex-member Simon Crowfoot on double bass. They totally lived up to their image and reputation, distorted guitar, sore throat vocals aaahhh music to my ears!

What exactly the Long Tall Texans were doing here nobody knew, they weren't billed and neither can they be described as a Psychobilly band, still variety is the spice of life as they say. Anyway, they gained my vote of approval as they were obviously playing for the fun of it as they didn't get paid! A lot of their set was made up of tracks from their excellent 'Sodbusters' album along with my favourite Texans track 'Get Back Wetback'. Their sound is pure rockin' excitement and they seemed to be enjoying themselves as much as the crowd were.

Biggest let downs of the festival were headliners Frenzy whose whole set seemed lifeless. Even what were once wild stompers such as 'Sweet Money' and 'Surfin' Bird' seemed dull and monotonous. They got nowhere near as good a reception as Torment or Batmobile except maybe from the die-hards at the front. Why such an excellent bass slapper plays stuff like this instead of showing off his amazing musical talent is a mystery. On the whole this festival was very well organised and was very successful.

After the article was published, I heard through the grapevine that Demented Are Go were not too happy with the review of their performance at the festival. This didn't stop them from being featured in a later issue. I never got any feedback about Frenzy's reaction to Howard's review but for some strange reason they were never featured in The Crazed although Steve Whitehouse the singer and bass player was always affable and chatty on the telephone. I never received any more reviews from Howard Piperides for reasons I never knew.

The Caravans.

 I had written to Bob Taylor lead guitarist of The Caravans, a rockin' band from Portsmouth who had become a regular feature at the Klub Foot. They had yet to release their debut album 'Easy Money' on Nervous Records. Bob provided me with a written biography of the band parts of which I used for my article. Here is Bob's written contribution dated 24/07/1987.

Line up:
> Mark Penington – Bass/lead vox.
> Bob Taylor – Lead Guitar.
> Lee Barnett – Drums.
> Brian Gillman – Rhythm Guitar.
> Darren Francis - Acoustic Guitar.

The band have been going for two years now, originally a four piece with drummer Pete Crowley but we split up in July 1985 for God knows what reason and reformed in November with new drummer Lee and third guitar Darren. We have played several London venues including Klub Foot, Dingwalls and Hammersmith Broadway. Supports include Restless, GuanaBatz, Frenzy, Batmobile, Highliners, The Meteors, Ray Campi and Levi Dexter. We play regularly at the Portsmouth club Basins who have a big rockin' band most Wednesday's and we have played often at both the Klub Foot and the Clay Pidgeon in Eastcote.

The band has a habit of usually going down well wherever they play not least because the drummer is a certified raving lunatic and the songs are fairly good since they interest Nervous, ABC and Northwood Records. The reasons for this are varied, firstly we have several good musicians who have been working together for a long time and know how to handle each other (touch wood) and secondly and probably most important we have a drummer and lead guitarist who are interested in styles of music far removed from Rockabilly but who how to incorporate these styles into Rockabilly without making something that sounds (too) strange. This incorporated with Mark's more traditional tastes make for some interesting, varied songs. In theory the main songwriters in the band are myself and Mark but when it comes down to it none of our songs would be what they are without the line-up that plays them.

We have twice played some foreign gigs, going twice to France, once to play with two other English bands – The Sureshots and Dave Phillips and the Hot Rod Gang and the other time to play in a converted barn in the middle of a field somewhere outside of Paris. We also did a mini tour of Holland supporting The Deltas in Utrecht.

We sell t-shirts at a fiver.

Wow, that dates it t-shirts for a fiver! Shortly after this contribution Bob left The Caravans to be replaced by Rich Caso who was a member of another rockin' Portsmouth band Get Smart. The Caravans were one of the few bands I featured twice, being interviewed face to face for a later issue.

The Coffin Nails.

I decided to interview The Coffin Nails who were also featured in issue one. I had been in correspondence with guitarist Humungus who was always helpful and kept me up to date with the latest news about the band. He informed me that Dave Ward had now become vocalist replacing Humungus who had previously taken over those duties after Tony Szajer left. He had also sent me details of The Coffin Nails fan club which he was hoping to launch, for £2.00 members would receive a free condom, a membership badge and card plus a six-monthly magazine. I don't know if this ever happened, but I didn't join. I'm not sure if the condom would have had the Coffin Nails logo on it! I managed to arrange an interview with the band at their next Klub Foot performance on 25th July 1987 which was conducted in their old trusted yellow van 'The Psycho Banana' parked outside the venue. New vocalist Dave seemed the most serious out of them all, without him the interview would probably have descended into chaos (more than it was). But it was an enjoyable experience and certainly an interview I look back on with a smile. The band had yet to release their debut album 'Ein Bier Bitte'.

The Coffin Nails the Psychobilly foursome who have been infecting many people who have seen them with their own brand of 'Psycho Disease'. The band hail from Reading and have become a regular band at the Klub Foot, where they ask the audience to lie on their backs and wreck! Anyway, the band went through some personal change at the beginning of the year firstly with original drummer Toby Griffin leaving the band to join The Meteors and also lead vocalist Tony Szajer leaving the band but this time not to join another band but to get married and move to Coventry. So, for a while the band were thrown into something of a turmoil. At one time lead guitarist Steve 'Humungus' Clarke was going to be vocalist but decided to let Dave Ward (who had previously replaced Toby on drums) take over the vacant vocalist position within the group. With Dave now on vocals this created a vacant place on drums, so after a couple of unsuccessful drummers they finally found someone who could create the right sound for the band which came in the form of Smurf (to anyone wondering why he's called Smurf it's not because he's blue or anything but as Humungus explains: "We don't know his real name".

So, with this new line up the band were ready to start gigging again and get back to inhabiting the stage at the Klub Foot, which by chance was where the following interview took place, well, outside the venue to be honest, with myself and the band all bundling into their 'Psycho Banana', which to the uneducated is the bands trusty yellow van. So, I decided to ask Dave, Humungus, Graham and Smurf some questions about The Coffin Nails. Prepare yourselves for a not very serious Coffin Nails interview ... ... AAAaaaRRRrrrGGGggHHHHH!!!!

First question, after Tony and Toby left did the band ever feel like calling it a day? Dave replies: "No, never. I joined when Toby left, I was on drums then Tony left and I started singing and we got this drummer called Mike who was just a complete dickhead". Graham intervenes: "And now we've got an even bigger dickhead". "Yeah Smurf" Dave replies. How did followers of the band react to Dave taking over Tony's place on vocals? Dave answers: "At the first gig we goes anybody who doesn't like the singer throw glasses and only one came so, I was quite happy". "Yeah, I threw it!" jokes Graham. Dave carries on: "No, it's been better than I thought it would be it's gone down well". Do you still get people asking where's Tony? "A lot of people ask after him" Graham answers. "Yeah, they ask what's happened to him and they ask what's he doing and why did he leave but they don't say is he coming back, which is good" replies Dave.

Most bands on the Rockabilly/Psychobilly scene have got double basses and as The Coffins Nails play on this scene and have got an electric bass, I wondered whether it had been harder for them to get accepted? Graham the bands bass player puts on a Vivian from the Young Ones (BBC television show) style voice and answers: "Yes I reckon". Humungus on hearing Graham's rather short answer decides to elaborate: "I think Graham can't play guitar!" on hearing this Graham puts on his Young Ones voice again and answers: "I think Steven's a fat bastard". I have a feeling it's going to be one of those interviews then all of a sudden Humungus gets up from the position he's been sitting in and crouches down and yells: "I've got my lager frenzy dance coming on!" and starts jumping up and down in the van, the whole van moves with the strain of the weight of the rather well-fed guitarist using the van as a trampoline. Some people who were watching the interview from outside the van whilst waiting for the Klub Foot doors to open walk away thinking that Humungus has gone insane. Then, just as quick as he started it, he quietly sits back down and appears calm again. I pondered what sort of question one can ask after an occurrence like this, on which I made the mistake of asking them the following ..... You once said that the difference between Rockabilly and Psychobilly is beer on this account would you describe yourselves as Psychobilly? On which the whole band answer: "Yeah, lager frenzy!", yep, you've guessed it Humungus is off again. He finally settles down and answers: "We're all alcholicers we do like a bit of alcohol now and again!", "Definitely, about every five minutes" Graham replies. "Which makes us Psychobilly's definitely" concludes Dave.

As we were originally attempting to talk about electric basses, would the band ever use a double bass? "The songs we've got sound better with an electric bass we think, possibly on a couple of songs not all the time" replies Dave. "The sensible one of the band" as Humungus explains.

As we were at the Klub Foot, I asked the band what they thought of their contribution on the Klub Foot video: "I thought there wasn't enough of me really" answers Humungus, "I don't care put it down right if anyone asks I was actually sober on the video!" replies Graham, explaining his rather "Where am I?" expression on the video. If it wasn't for Psychobilly would the Coffin Nails have been a Rockabilly band? There's a slight silence: "That's a hard one, that is" says Graham, Dave then takes up the point: "I think we'd definitely be a Rockabilly band opposed to a Punk band, we'd go that side of it opposed to the Punk side". So, who influences your music then? Dave suddenly points at Humungus: "Look at him who does it look like? ..... Paul Fenech, The Meteors". "He's, my Dad" jokes Humungus.

I remember reading once that the band had had interest from Hollands RockHouse Records, I wondered whether it was true?

"They were once" answers Humungus, "We've got a deal with Nervous Records now" butts in Dave. So, how did that happen? Dave explains: "I phoned them up 'cos I'm cool". "No, no, no" interjects Humungus, correcting Dave who continues: "I wrote them a letter and they said yes, we're pretty interested and wanted a live tape, so we sent them a live tape and he phoned me up and said 'How do you fancy doing an album?' and we got a deal with Nervous". Sounds easy, eh? But Nervous weren't originally that interested in the band, they've waited for them to become more experienced, and the wait has been worth it for the band.

Like many other Rockabilly/Psychobilly bands the coverage of the band in the music press has been virtually non-existent, why does the music press ignore Rockabilly and Psychobilly? Dave answers: "Because they hold people like The Sex Pistols and anything that challenges commercial music, and they sort of put The Sex Pistols up on a pedestal and anyone who challenges that is ignored now and Psychobilly has done that and they choose to ignore it 'cos they love The Sex Pistols so much and they reckon Punk was a time when people were rebelling and now it's all over". "Here, here David" joke the band regarding Dave's serious answer.

What can we expect from The Coffin Nails in the future? Humungus: "To make money". Dave: "Lots of money, lots of records". Graham: "Lots of money, lots of little blond groupies round the back". Humungus then looks at Smurf the bands rather silent drummer: "Smurf, what have you got planned for the future?", Smurf looks up and answers: "To make lots of money". "I said that" says Humungus (who's called Humungus because that's what Pip of the GuanaBatz said he looked like when he first saw him), Dave also says: "Good answer Smurf". "Good one" Graham jokes. "We just want to get bigger basically" replies Dave. "Smurf says he wants to go to America" says Graham, Humungus takes up the point: "Dave keeps on telling us we might be touring America, but I think he might be making it up". "No, I'm not!" answers Dave. So, you wouldn't mind making it in America? "I'll make it anyway baby" jokes Graham, Dave explains: "I think it would be easier making it in America than over here". Graham: "Why are their beds bigger?", Dave continues: "'Cos over here there's so many Psychobilly bands it's not had its day but with bands like The Meteors about they're at the top and it's going to be very difficult for bands like us to get up with them, but in America it might be easier. (looking at my questions) Is that it?" on finding out it was the whole band shout out: "Ask us some more!", Humungus: "Ask why Smurf never says nothing ...... because he's still a virgin!".

I believe the band had enjoyed my interview, Humungus a few months later asked me if I wanted to interview them again, if the The Crazed had lasted for more than another two issues I expect another one would have been conducted. Dave later left the band to be replaced by Humungus on vocals. One of the first gigs to feature him in this new role was at The Klub Foot night at The Town and Country Club after the sad demise of the Clarendon Hotel (more of that later). After their performance Humungus asked me what I thought of the new line up, I must be honest I was impressed as he seemed to have smoothly and effortlessly moved into the new role and had put on a good show. He seemed pleased with my observation; it was also flattering to be asked. Band members like Humungus helped The Crazed due to always being approachable, helpful and enthusiastic.

The Krewmen.

I had managed to obtain the telephone number of Reg The Krewmen's manager, so, armed with a pocketful of coins I made my way to the phone box which I unofficially used as my office, it was in a quiet area and was rarely used. I remember the annoyance I felt when on the rare occasion somebody was using it, I would storm off on my pushbike to find another phone box. I was impatient and had no time to wait as I had interviews to arrange and information about the scene to learn, which to me at the time was of high importance. I rang the deep voiced Reg and managed to arrange an interview with the band on 29th May or June 1987 (my paperwork records the two dates) at Canterbury College where they would be supporting the GuanaBatz.

I caught the train to Canterbury and made my way to the college with my trusted tape recorder, Kodak Disc camera and a set of questions for the band and also some for The GuanaBatz in the hope they might agree to an interview, which had worked rather well with The Meteors at the Fractured gig. Upon entering the part of the college, they would be playing I met both bands including The Krewmen's manager Reg and immediately felt at ease, both bands seemed comfortable and friendly in each other's company, creating a relaxed atmosphere, great conditions for an interview. Before the interview I spoke to Krewmen guitarist Tony McMillan who was very amenable and chatty. It seemed an informative interview would soon be conducted, that is until I pressed the red record button on my tape recorder and Tony's demeanour changed, he became a lot more guarded and seemed a little uncomfortable having to answer my questions along with the other members of his band. But with sheer determination I proceeded with the interview.

After having a drastic line-up change being that Tony McMillan is the only member left from their previous line up, The Krewmen decided it was time to change their music as well. They wanted to play more contemporary music instead of the traditional Rockabilly and Rhythm and Blues that the previous line ups had. So, with a load of tunes and lyrics in their heads, Tony and new vocalist Mark Cole put their songs into action along with Jason Thornton (who took over Tony's place on the double bass as he moved onto guitar) and Dominic Parr who drums up the frantic beat. Lost Moment Records who had previously signed up a previous Krewmen line up were impressed by the new sound and decided an album was needed. Off went the lads to a recording studio in Reading out of which the band's debut album 'Adventures of The Krewmen' came. Lost Moment on hearing the album soon put the band back into the recording studio to record a follow up album. This came in the form of 'Sweet Dreams' which proved to be a vast improvement. Sweet Dreams entered the UK Independent charts and along with a support slot on the GuanaBatz recent tour around the country have made The Krewmen a popular band on the gigging circuit with their frantic live act.

I decided to ask the band a few questions. I wondered how the original fans of the previous line ups reacted to the new look and sound, "What fans?" replies slap bassist Jason. Tony realising, he was in the previous lines ups ignores the bassist's comments and explains: "Most of them prefer the new stuff, we had a few that moaned about it. We done a gig in Reading someone walked in and walked out when he heard us 'cos he came to see the Blues stuff and that. But on the whole, it's been alright, really people have accepted it". But as the group changed so much why did you keep the name The Krewmen? Tony explains: "A lot of people knew the name of The Krewmen if we had got a new name, we'd have had to start from scratch again, so we just carried on".

On previous records with an earlier line up (these being two singles and a twelve-inch e.p. on Lost Moment) Tony played bass. I asked why did he move onto guitar? "I didn't!" replies Dominic the bands drummer. The band break into laughter at the bearded drummer's joke (?) when the laughter dies down Tony finally answers the question: "It was hard to find a guitarist to do this stuff as I was writing the songs on guitar, and it was hard to find a guitarist to do it the way I wanted it". Jason who filled Tony's place in the new line up replies: "It's hard to find a good and fast enough bass player".

After having various lines ups (I found out there had been three in all) I wondered if the band had now found what they'd been looking for musically? "Indubitably" Tony replies, "All apart from Jason". The band seem to find themselves very popular abroad as their first album sold ten thousand copies and most of them were sales from abroad. "We're surprised really how popular we are out there" explains Tony. The band have even found interest from America as they've recorded a video of 'Night Shift Blues' (from their first album) for M.T.V. Reg the bands manager explains how that came about: "It came from an advert in Sounds looking for bands, we applied among four hundred others and after about two months they fixed a date" and the band started filming. The video consists of the band performing the song along with clips of the band: "Messing around Basingstoke where we come from". Whether the video will be shown in the UK remains to be seen (no pun intended).

The Krewmen also supported the GuanaBatz on the Batz tour of England which certainly helped record sales for The Krewmen 'Sweet Dreams' album. "It's gone really well" explains Tony. "Diddle nicks all the birds, Pip nicks all the food" replies vocalist Mark Cole describing the Batz. "They're a lovely bunch of lads" concludes Jason, "Apart from Pip when he gets hungry" adds Dominic quickly finishing his sandwich.

How much do the band think their 'Sweet Dreams' album differs from the first? Dominic: "There's a hell of a lot of difference really". Jason: "It's a lot more fuller". Tony: "It's more like our own style whereas the other one you could probably say it sounds like so and so or whatever, it's more our own sort of thing". I also notice that the band produce their own records "We don't allow any outside influence at all" explains Tony. With this sort of arrangement, I wondered how well the band get on with their record company Lost Moment who have also released records by The Rattlers and as previously stated an earlier Krewmen line up. The band reply that they are very pleased with their relationship with Lost Moment, as long as the band come up with the goods the record company are pleased.

For the future Tony explains that The Krewmen will: "Do some gigs, start working on another album, we're getting the material ready for it. It'll be ready after Christmas probably". Jason sums up what he wants from being a member of The Krewmen in one sentence: "Sex, drugs and Rock 'n' Roll".

Mark Cole left the band before the interview was published in issue two. The band informed me they were looking for a new vocalist and asked me to include an advert for a new one in the fanzine, which resulted in a 'stop press' news alert on page two which included a telephone number for any potential hopefuls. I don't know how much interest this generated as Tony McMillan later took over the vocal duties and still managed to continue to build the bands popularity, especially abroad.

GuanaBatz.

With the GuanaBatz still hanging around after The Krewmen's interview and a burning list of questions for them in my pocket, it seemed too good an opportunity to miss. Stuart Osbourne the bands guitarist was sitting outside the room where the gig was to be. The rest of the band must have still been inside tuning up or maybe Pip was on the search for food! Stuart seemed approachable and agreed to be interviewed which was another huge addition for issue two. The Batz being arguably the second biggest band on the Psychobilly scene at the time, having recorded four John Peel sessions for his legendary Radio One show and whose record releases easily entered the independent charts. They along with The Meteors were a huge influence for many bands on the Psychobilly scene along with vocalist Pip's charismatic stage presence, whose outgoing personality also managed to be captured on their records. They were featured on the first 'Stomping at The Klub Foot' album, turning the theme tune for the t.v. show 'Joe 90' into a Psychobilly classic. Last time I had seen the Batz was at the Angel Centre in Tonbridge never at the time thinking I would be hanging out with them in Canterbury. The band even had their own fan club which included sending members a signed photo of themselves. With Stuart sitting comfortably and no longer having my fake cockney accent I had used during my interview with The Meteors I opened my list of questions. Here it is.

Held down to being interviewed at last! One of the most popular rockin' bands around, the GuanaBatz. They have impressed many people with their unique interpretation of the music. When they first began in 1982, they were originally compared with The Meteors (as there weren't too many Psychobilly bands around at that time, even The Sting-Rays were compared to The Meteors then), but since then they have matured their music so when you hear it you immediately know it's the GuanaBatz distinctive sound and nobody else's. The band have played various gigs around the country and have built up a very loyal nationwide following. All of their record releases chartered in the indie charts, their 'Loan Sharks' album getting to number two in the indie album charts. The Batz have also recorded a few sessions for the John Peel show on Radio One. But, still after all this the music press virtually ignores them, labelling them as a Rockabilly band and putting them aside until the music comes back into vogue again. Diddle drummer of the band doesn't appear to be that bothered about it though as he claims that all the music paper journalists are "Failed musicians anyway" (I wonder what he thinks of fanzine writers, funny I never bothered to ask). After all this under exposure from the press I thought it was about time an interview with the GuanaBatz for The Crazed was needed. So just before they were due to go on stage, I asked Stuart Osbourne, guitarist of the band and main songwriter some questions, we were also joined by GuanaBatz mascot dog Mutley.

I decided to begin the interview asking Stuart about the Batz 'Live Over London' album, does he think it's a good interpretation of a Batz gig? "Yes, I do, I think it's very good, not just from the technical side of it but I think it turned out very well, much better than the 'Stomping at The Klub Foot' album. I mean punters may not like it, but you never know, but I think it's the best recording we've done yet". Why didn't Diddle play at the original recording of it? "He went out to a pub' cos he likes going to pubs does Diddle and he ran into a gang of Soul Boys with his mates and they didn't want any trouble so they made a hasty retreat. Diddle fell over and landed on a glass and slashed all his wrist so there was no way he could play with stiches in his arm, so we had to get Ginger to play". Ginger used to drum for the Batz awhile back? "Yes, that's right but we had a bit of trouble with Ginger at the time 'cos he had a few personal problems and he wasn't very reliable unfortunately, so we had to get Dave back" (more of that later on).

Although the two nights still went ahead for the recording of the album the band agreed that they had to re-record the album this time with Diddle. The only difference being that this time the GuanaBatz weren't headlining the gig as they previously had and also did not appear as the GuanaBatz on the bill but under a pseudonym of Pip and The Pip Dogs. Why was this? I ask Stuart: "That was because we couldn't really appear as the GuanaBatz supporting 999 at the Klub Foot 'cos it wouldn't have looked right and we had to get a fast recording anyway and there wasn't enough time basically to do another Klub Foot under our own name, so we just did that for the sake of the recording". Is all the re-recording featured on the album? "Yeah, there's one track with Ginger from the first two nights but what we have done is we've overdubbed the cheering from the first two nights onto that night, so there's no 999 crowd on there it's all the crowd from the first two nights. So basically, everyone that was there the first two nights is on the album although that's not the gig they were at". Confusing stuff, eh? But still after all that the album is a worthwhile purchase and features tracks such as King Rat and Loan Sharks played in the atmosphere that suits them best, live.

Just before the 'Live Over London' album was released Jettisoundz released a live video of the Batz, half of it recorded from a gig the Batz played at the Klub Foot this year and the other half is taken from a gig the Batz played in Nottingham in 1984, Stu explains his views on the tape: "The first twenty minutes of it from the Klub Foot is quite good but then when they use the old stuff you can tell the difference in the band, the bands improved in that time and it really sticks out". The video does include a couple of collectable tracks from the 1984 gig these being the moody 'Zombie Walk' and the frantic 'Get Along' both of which are currently unreleased record wise.

The bands 'Loan Sharks' album went shooting up the independent charts when it was released, were the band surprised at the success of the album? "Well, gauging the success of the first album we was hoping to sell a few more copies than that, but I was surprised at the response we got for it, being that the older more established fans we got really liked it but the younger generation didn't like it they said it wasn't sort of fast enough, it wasn't Psychobilly enough which was true 'cos we was trying to sort of broaden our horizons a bit but it was okay. It was a definite improvement on 'Held Down to Vinyl' but I think the next album will be an improvement on the 'Loan Sharks' album". Some people were disappointed there were only six Batz compositions on it, why were there so many cover versions on it? "I wrote more songs than that. I wrote originally nine, but we dropped some of them 'cos they didn't work. So, that's basically it we dropped three of them. What people don't realise is that we got managers of record companies which are pressurising you into recording an album in three months' time and that's a deadline, so if you screw up on a couple of songs and you have to drop them then there's no other choice but to put on a few covers".

The title track of the album 'Loan Sharks' was released as a single, the b-side featured another track off the album and there was no picture cover for the single. Stuart explains why it was released: "That wasn't actually supposed to be a general release, that was a special for the radio because most daytime disc jockeys don't play album tracks and they don't play 12" singles either so we had to release it as a single to get any chance of radio play. Because when you write off to America and big places like that want to know if you're on British radio and it carries a lot of weight if you are. So, it's basically we just tried to get on the radio, and it wasn't supposed to be a general release thing". So, were you disappointed it was generally released? "Oh yeah, well that was just to pay for the pressing, so it's like a very rare collector's item now of the GuanaBatz". Has it been deleted? "Yeah, there was only like a thousand copies made, very rare that is. I haven't even got one". Another track taken off the 'Loan Sharks' album was the Bruce Springsteen cover 'I'm on Fire', I wondered if the Batz had any contact from the Boss about their cover version of his composition? "No, none at all". Would Stuart want any though? "Wouldn't mind to hear what his reactions were".

As the Batz covered 'I'm on Fire' which was a hit in the national charts for Bruce Springsteen would they like to be a chart band? Stuart answers: "I wouldn't mind being a chart band if we could do what we're doing now", say a major label said you couldn't do the sort of music you are doing now and told you to change it around in terms of chart success? "It depends on whether I want to retire at the end of the year really because that's how long you are going to last, it's such a short scope. When you sign onto a major unless you're going to get like five million pounds for it which you can retire for the rest of your life on or get another business or something there's no point, you might as well stay as you are with a good following".

At one time during the Batz past they had a female saxophonist, I wondered what happened to her? "She got sacked" Why? Stuart explains: "It was basically like it put the group up to five members which we had to pay. So, there was five instead of four which dropped the wages down quite a bit, less economical to do gigs for us 'cos we don't have jobs and also she was a very limited saxophone player. So, it just came down to economics, not fitting in the group well, costing too much to do and we weren't getting much reward for doing it. Not many people liked it, so we gave her the chop". Why did you feel the need to get a saxophonist in? "Basically, because there was so many groups at the time with guitar, singer, double bass and a set of drums that we thought it would make us a bit different from everyone else but it just seems that everyone has got a saxophonist at the moment and there's so many groups about with it that I'm glad we didn't stick with that idea for long".

Keeping on the subject of previous band members, I enquire as to what happened to their original (electric) bass player Mick White: "We fell out with him, I think that's about the politest way you could say it. We just got fed up with his attitude and he was trying to run the group because he had been in The Meteors and he knew best type thing and we just got fed up with him so we dropped him. He was the GuanaBatz was like his attitude, bad feeling was just building up, it started to get on everyone's nerves. He kept butting in the whole time and like he was a total idiot anyway, not a very good bass player". Is that why Diddle left the band due to Mick departing? "Mick and Dave were good friends since way back, they go back a long way, they were at school together and I think Mick just made Diddle feel that he was obliged to stick with him, so he left us for that reason and then realised it was a mistake after two months and asked to re-join us which worked out fine in the end".

How did you find Sam Sardi who replaced Mick and this time introduced a double bass to the group? Stu explains: "When Ginger left The Meteors he approached us and said I hear you've got trouble with Mick and Dave do you want us to come in, with me and Sam and start the Batz again and we said yeah fine, so that was basically it, because they were interested in reforming some sort of group. Sam's brother Steve was married with a kid at the time so that ruled him out as the guitarist and this chap Lester they used to have in The Ricochets he got on their nerves, so they sacked him and they was just looking for a guitarist and vocalist. It just fitted in, it just fell into place, it wasn't planned intentionally or anything it just came out that way, it was really strange". To the uneducated Sam and Ginger used to be in The Ricochets along with Sam's brother Steve and a vocalist called Lester Jones.

What made the Batz decide to use a slap bass as previously they had an electric bass? "The only reason we started off with the electric bass was because we couldn't find a double bass. There's a bloke around my way called Mick Wigfall, I did a few songs with him but he didn't turn out very well so we dropped him and then got another electric bass player. It was just basically for the lack of bass players, there didn't seem to be enough bass players to go round in London". So, if you could have got a double bass player "He'd have been in from the start". Mutley decides to make a comment, not wanting to be outdone Stuart promptly shuts the other wisely silent dog up.

As the Batz have now released three albums and various singles I wondered if there was any record that they regret recording? Stuart answers: "I regret recording 'Held Down to Vinyl', I wished we'd saved all that material 'til we'd got the right sound for the group because there was so much material that is just wasted 'cos it sounds so bad, weak and feeble on that album. Apart from that everything else is fine. It was just that album, so much work went into that one 'cos that was the first album we did and there was like two year's work gone into it and it was just like thrown away". So, you weren't keen on the production of it? "No, it was just really bad 'cos we went into a studio in Chelsea, and they didn't have enough microphones to mic everything up properly, so I had to overdub the guitar, we just couldn't get a good sound because of the studio basically".

As the GuanaBatz new recordings aren't specifically Psychobilly, I asked Stuart what he thought of the Psychobilly tag that seems to be restricting the Batz credibility with the music press: "Well, it's a lot better than being called a Rockabilly/Rock 'n' Roll group, there's a lot more interest in Psychobilly than there is in rockin' stuff at the moment. Well, if that's what people want to call us then that's fine everyone's happy". But would you like the Batz to be remembered as being a Psychobilly band? "Well, if that's the only thing I'm going to be remembered by I suppose it's better than nothing".

During the Batz steady rise in the rockin' scene many bands have picked up their double bass's, guitars and drums and hoped to follow in their footsteps, so, what bands does Stuart tip for the top for the future? "Well, who is there about at the moment? Wigsville Spliffs there's a possibility they might get on, they're good musicians and that. A group which is totally not Psychobilly which is going to get big is Fourteen Karat Soul, one day they'll get big. Howlin' Wilf and The Vee Jays I think they've got a future as well because I notice Dr Feelgood is starting to play bigger venues, so that sort of music scenes definitely going to get big again, there's no one who plays it like Howlin' Wilf do, they're brilliant". For the future the Batz themselves wish to keep their loyal following, as Stuart explains: "We got a good following around the country which we're really pleased people make the effort to come and see us instead of sitting indoors playing a record or listening to a bootleg! Or.... reading The Crazed. We're just pleased that people make the effort to come and see us and it couldn't be better for us at the moment. The only other thing we want to happen is to go to America, if we get big in America that would be my fantasy come true". Backing Bruce Springsteen? "No, Bruce Springsteen backing us".

Pip emerged after the interview and asked: "Want to do the interview?" both Stuart and I answered that it had already been done much to his disappointment. I still wonder why I didn't interview Pip as well, maybe not enough tape left or possibly it was because Stuart gave such comprehensive answers, I had what I needed for a good write up. Sam Sardi the bands double bass player also showed interest in an interview although not about the band but his car collection, I was too much into the music to take him up on that. I later met Stuart again at the Klub Foot, he was in the bar area, I said hello, he looked at me with no recognition. "I interviewed you for my fanzine The Crazed" I embarrassingly said, he was with a female companion who remembered the interview, she prompted him, "Oh yeah, you alright" he finally answered. In 2021 I met Stuart again at a gig, this time he stated that he remembered the interview in Canterbury, and we had a good discussion and a pint about the rockin'old days. He agreed to an interview for this book, and it was left that that I would contact him to arrange one, but unfortunately, when it came to arranging it he never responded back, maybe he forgot about the original Crazed interview again. The rest of the band seemed to recognise me, I remember standing with them in the bar downstairs at the The Clarendon Hotel on a Klub Foot night along with Jeroen Haamers of Batmobile (ridiculously I never spoke to Jereon about arranging an interview for The Crazed) the bar was packed with Psychobilly's and there I was with the Batz and Batmobile how can I describe the feeling? I suggested to Pip about producing a fanzine solely about the Batz called (wait for it) The Batzine, he laughed and replied: "No one will read it!". I also had a good conversation with Diddle outside the legendary venue talking about how Psychobilly's with their painted quiffs and shaven sides fare at job interviews. Diddle later left the band to be replaced by Jonny Bowler who played double bass in a rockin' band called Get Smart. Pip moved to America and Diddle is sadly no longer with us.

Reader's section.

I had decided to include a reader's section featuring edited versions from some of the correspondence I had started to receive. This managed to fill a whole page of the fanzine and also included a drawing sent in by Simon Minall from Cornwall, who voiced his disappointment when I met him whilst talking to a few Psychobilly's outside the Klub Foot that his contribution had been minimized to fit onto the page. I had also used comments from what band members had said to me either on the phone or in person.

I introduced the page with the following:

This page readers is your page, if you've got any comments or anything you want to send in, I'll sort through it all and include the ones I've chosen. Here's a few comments, contributions and drawings I received from issue one.

Just writing to congratulate you on a brilliant mag.
Andrew Gardner, correct Crazed reader, Doncaster, S. Yorks.

I don't want missed it!
Hinault Dimitri, confused Crazed reader, France.

"Take a photograph of me reading it!".
Pip of the GuanaBatz, proud Crazed reader

At last, a Psycho mag that's going to get somewhere.
Slops, complimentary Crazed reader, Herts.

I was impressed.
Humungus of The Coffin Nails and avid Crazed reader.

I would like to congratulate you on having the initiative to top an as yet unrecognised market. It's good to see that there is someone with the ability to go where no music press has gone and actually

pay service to Psychobilly/Rockabilly music!
Bod, serious Crazed reader, Bothwell, Scotland.

I think it's very well presented. I like the interview with The Coffin Nails that was a good idea.
Toby 'Jug' Griffin, Meteors drummer and impressed Crazed reader.

Andy Gardner from Doncaster S. Yorks sent in a contribution about The Long Tall Texans:

I have some info to add to your Long Tall Texans feature. I got the info myself direct from the boys! The name comes from an old banjo Blue Grass song of the thirties/forties which is played at half the speed the Texans do it at! It has been recorded by people such as Beach Boys, Wilko Johnson, Skiff Skats and Hank Wangford. Although it is not known who did the original.

Slops from Herts sent in a Klub Foot gig review from the 25th July 1987, this is a slightly longer version than the printed version in issue two:

I hope you don't mind but I took the liberty of sending you a review of the Batmobile gig at the Klub Foot on July 25th :- Well, it was my first visit to the Klub Foot since Christmas and what a welcome return I had. Five excellent bands wrenching their guts out for us bloodthirsty onlookers. I'd been watching a few daring lads lobbing their finest pints of finest London ale at passing motorists, so by the time I was inside The Nitros were already bursting forth, an exciting threesome possibly the best band of the night for me. An exhilarating combination of Blues and Rockabilly (including a version of Summertime) that had many of us tapping our feet.

Then came Fractured a disappointing band following in the footsteps of Restless and coming from the deep depths of Tunbridge Wells, they were to blame for getting everyone wrecking. I saw a couple of arguments and a scuffle at the back while they were on. They did a good version of Big Bad John though.

The Coffin Nails were very popular as always. They did most of the tried and tested songs such as Psycho Disease and Let's Wreck as well as a Psycho version of Greased Lightnin' and as usual ole Steve on guitar was larking about and adding his own personal touches to the set.

Torment, this is the first time I've seen this West County trio it must be admitted and to be honest it took them a while to get going, I thought. However, they are firm favourites (most people will have both records in their collection including me) and they did most of their known classic stuff including Mystery Man, Psyclops Carnival and Torment plus their own version of Cry or Die. Simon B has now abandoned his angular quiff but Simon C on bass still has his six-inch luminous orange beauty and still kept his cooler than cool stance despite losing his specs halfway through.

Then the band everyone was waiting for. A lot of Germans and Dutch had come over to see Batmobile and they weren't disappointed. Donned in Stoneage costume they hammered out old classics like Slappin' Suspenders, Bat Attack, Transylvanian Express and Bamboo Land with ole Eric slapping the daylights out of his paint splattered bass and handing out plastic caveman clubs.

So, a good night as always. The Nitros will be famous one day, well, I'll be first in the queue to buy their records and if you do get the chance to see The Coffin Nails or Batmobile then go, it'll be worth your while.

Reading it now, I wish I had included other Klub Foot reviews, but at the time reviewing gigs for me wasn't a priority. Anyway, I often had had a few pints of whatever they served behind the bar and couldn't always remember everything clearly the next day. At least Slops had remained sober enough to write a good review about another legendary night in Hammersmith.

Toby 'Jug' Griffin drummer of The Meteors had also written to me providing me with the following information regarding The Meteors: "We will be doing a video of one of our live gigs and we are presently recording our new album (Don't Touch the Bang Bang Fruit) and have finished the single (Go Buddy Go). We'll also be touring Germany or England in June (I think). I'll let you know. I think that you should give the 'zine a cover that will make it stand out more, I've enclosed one idea" he signed off the letter Jug. He was very diplomatic how he indirectly told me that he was not overkeen on the cover and included a design he had created for a new logo for The Crazed, I was very impressed and included it on the cover of issue two.

Kevin Haynes the drummer from Torment whom I had interviewed for issue one also took pity on the ropey issue one cover and agreed to provide one of his designs for issue two, the design he sent me featured a three-piece Psychobilly band playing guitar, drums and double bass. This was a boost for The Crazed as Kevin also designed record sleeves for Nervous Records. This arrangement with Kevin lasted for the duration of The Crazed and he contributed some great designs which certainly did make the fanzine stand out more. What a step up from the cover of issue one, instead of a rushed design by me issue two featured a logo by the drummer of The Meteors and the cover illustration provided by the drummer from Torment. Not a bad achievement for the second issue, I was obviously getting noticed and more importantly my typed-up interviews were getting read. Even before issue two was released people within the scene were staring to take notice.

The Wigsville Spliffs top tens.

The Wigsville Spliffs provided me with their favourite top ten records, continuing the theme started with issue one:

Mike Lister: Bass

       The Cat –Rod Willis
       Big Green Car-The Polecats
       Fujiyama Mama-Pearl Harbour
       Who Slapped John-Gene Vincent
       Devil's Guitar-GuanaBatz
       Baby Please Don't Go-Restless
       BambooLand-Batmobile
       Liberator-Spear of Destiny
       Vanish Without a Trace –Restless
       Big Noise from Winetka-Bob Crosby.

Ian Aitken: Vocals and lead guitar

       Hold Me, Hug Me, Rock Me-Gene Vincent
       Cat Squirrel-Dr. Ross
       I Smell a Rat-Young Jessie
       You Crazy Gal You-Buzz and The Flyers
       After Midnight-Restless
       Mumblin' Guitar-Bo Diddley
       My Baby Don't Rock-Luke McDaniel
       Miss Pearl-Jimmy Wages
       Jump Around-The Stargazers
       The Girl Can't Help It- Little Richard

Danny Mowl: Drums

       Robot Riot-Frenzy
       Rock the Casbah-The Clash
       Surfin' Bird-The Trashmen

Teenage Cutie-Eddie Cochran
Wound Up-Frenzy
Edge on You-Restless
Ah, Poor Little Baby- Billy Craddock
Love Me-The Phantom
Uncle Sam-Torment
Trapped Love-Keith Courvale

Printing issue 2 and the written introduction.

Before writing the introduction, I had to seek out a shop to hopefully print The Crazed correctly on A5 size pages and not on A4 as had mistakenly happened with issue one. The place that had printed issue one had now closed (no surprise there) and a new printing shop had recently opened locally. I got a quote which would mean a slight increase in price of the fanzine and was told I could choose a coloured paper for the cover, which would make it a little more visually appealing. I chose a light blue paper. Tim, who worked in the shop (still does) took an interest in helping with the whole process and would also fold and staple the pages together. There were no staples in issue one! I also decided to print some more flyers which would kindly be distributed with Nervous Records, Zorch News mail out. This flyer would now proudly feature photos of both The Meteors and GuanaBatz, I was going Psychobilly big time.

With all this excitement and after a helluava lot of typing and transcribing I was now ready to write the introduction, to an issue which I thought was a big improvement from issue one:

Hallo ye Crazed people!

We're back again, firstly I'd like to apologise for the increase in price and decrease in size of the zine but this is due to the place where I got issue one printed closing down and this is the cheapest alternative I could find, so I'm sorry about that. But, apart from that I hope you enjoy this issue. As you can see the style of the zine has changed a bit, I hope you like it. I've introduced a reader's page and some live reviews. If you've got any comments then send them into the Raucous Records address (written above) and they will pass them onto me. Anyway, I hope you enjoy this issue.

I had also prior to printing received news from The Krewmen which I included on the intro page as a 'stop press' small feature:

Mark Cole of The Krewmen has left the band due to various reasons and the band are now looking for a new vocalist.

I also included a contact telephone number for them.

Printing issue 2.

Issue two was now completed and ready to be printed. With the original pages carefully placed into a bag off I proudly went to the printing shop. I hoped that the whole look and style of this issue would appear as good as Tim the printer had described. So, leaving all my hard work including all those typed out pages with photos and designs stuck onto them with him I waited whilst it all got printed and collated. I returned a few days later and Tim pointed to some boxes which were full of a couple of hundred copies of issue two, he showed me a copy, I was really impressed, the smaller size and the light blue cover was exactly how I had hoped it would look, more compact and as professional as I could achieve with my limited skills. I hoped that the readers would agree. I knew by including interviews with the two biggest bands on the scene The Meteors and GuanaBatz it would attract some attention. The flyers also looked good as well. Now I had to send them to my distributor Raucous Records and the flyers to Roy Williams from Nervous Records. The Crazed issue two would soon be unleashed onto an unsuspecting Psychobilly world!

This issue was my favourite out of all the four. I feel the content, design and enthusiasm that went into it was the closest to reach my expectations. Although there was still very good content to come in the next two issues, arguably issue two was the best. It sold the most as well. When I spoke to people outside the Klub Foot before the doors opened some were aware of the zine or had bought and read a copy. I could ring record companies such as ID/ABC and they would provide me news about their bands and send me promo photos. Roy Williams would chat with me inside the venue as would Pete Gage who produced some of the bands and also managed Restless. Didn't always work though as Jamie from ID showed no interest in acknowledging me when he was on the door of The Klub Foot ,when I informed him I was on the guest list for one of the bands, "We spoke on the phone last week" I confidently said, remembering a friendly informative call we previously had, "I take so many calls, I don't remember them all" he dismissively replied. Apart from that, The Crazed seemed to be building on its momentum. My initial mission to interview the bands and get known on the scene seemed to be working.

Readers' letters.

The letters I received from the readers regarding issue two were positive, here is an example:

I received issue 2 of The Crazed the other day and was stirred to write to you, the mag was summed up in one word BRILLIANT! I prefer the layout and style of no. 2 as well as the size and well worth (I think) 10p extra. I thought the Batz interview came across well as did The Meteors one. How about an interview with Restless in the near future? Keep it up!

Just got your issue of The Crazed 2. Much more in it than the last one. I saw in The Crazed you got an interview with P. Paul Fenech. I have written everywhere looking for information on The Meteors and Demented Are Go but got nothing. If you could give me an address for information. I would be grateful.

Can you please send the 3rd issue of The Crazed. Is the new Meteors video out yet? As Jettiisoundz have not yet advertised it.

Just had to write to say how great The Crazed is, real informative and in-depth interviews at last. Being stuck out of the way up North means you hear less with being well out of the scene. We don't get many chances to see bands live and records in the shops are scarce. Any chance of getting an interview with The Highliners, Ginger Meadham's latest band must surely go far, what with their catchy songs, great stage image and tv appearances to boot, how can they fail? Also, how about news of releases and more reviews.

Just writing to congratulate you on a superb mag, it's about time somebody made a mag about Psychobilly. The only thing is there any chance of making it bigger because I don't think I would mind paying a bit extra because where else can they find out the info they need. Keep up the good work.

Interesting letter from reader.

Here is a rather entertaining and informative (about the Loughborough scene) letter I received after issue two (I did have suspicions who wrote it) it is dated 04/06/1988 and is from a certain Leopold Wolfen from Wolfsville!.

'The first issue of The Crazed was quite good but didn't seem to have much in it. I still sent for issue 2 expecting it to be like issue 1, but it is brilliant, the best mag I've read. It is really well presented and packed with information a great improvement on issue 1. The size and illustrations are much better. I hope to see issue 3 very soon. Why don't you cover some of the new bands coming out that are hardly known this would be very interesting to me. There are two bands on Raucous Records that are not very well known. I would like to know more about them. They are Spellbound and The Griswalds. Coming from Loughborough (I don't) you must have seen The Cliffhangers a Rockin' trio who have done various gigs. I saw them on their debut with The Go-Katz brilliant young band also from Loughborough at Loughborough University they were really crap, then but have come a long way since then and now are a good wild band. They played with another young band not so long ago at Loughborough Casablanca Club called The Hellraisers. Their first gig was at Casablanca with The Cliffhangers and they sounded as good if not better than The Cliffs, it's just that they played for half an hour on stage and did lots of covers. The second time I saw them at Casablanca they were much better but the bass was electric and didn't sound as good as a double probably would. The Go-Katz are another band I would like to read more about. They were in issue 1. I've been to see them quite a few times including their first gig at The Mad Cat in Loughborough with Torment. They sounded quite good but Bad Moon was spoilt by the singing which was way out of key, I've also got this track on a demo and it's not very good on there either. All their own tracks are brilliant. Their debut E.P. on Raucous Records was brilliant and a must have for any Rockin' Psycho collection. Thanks for a great mag.'

Although it is always complimentary receiving correspondence and feedback, I was always of the old Punk mentality of do it yourself. Filling a whole page with reader's letters, comments and drawings like issue two was not repeated for the next two issues. A fair bit of mail wanted contact details of certain bands, my only contact details at the time were the same resources as theirs, records sleeves or mails out. Meeting bands such as The Meteors and GuanaBatz meant having to physically ask them for an interview, I had no correspondence details for them. I suppose the readers also assumed I knew about release dates of records and tours as well, which is quite likely as I had more access to the bands and labels, but the information could become outdated very quickly when put into print. With these requests for information about certain bands, I should have asked for commission from them. I also received a query from a Rockin' company in Sweden enquiring about advertising rates, I had no idea about anything like that and in my naivety wasn't interested in selling space in The Crazed.

Wieze Psychobilly Festival 1987.

Roy Williams under his infamous alias Captain Zorch sent me a gig review of the Psycho Festival in Wieze, Belgium 16th and 17th October 1987:

Second Belgian Psycho Festival.

The second festival of this type took place on October this year at Wieze. For those who don't know Wieze is a little Belgium town where a huge beer festival is held. That was the week before the festival but there was no fear of running out of liquid refreshment since the hall where the festival took place had a brewery at one end! This was on the same weekend as the famous storm in Southern England so my flight over was rather bumpy. I made the last leg of the journey on a special Psycho bus laid on by the promoter. The cassette machine in the bus chewed up my Cramps cassette, so it was a bad start for me!

We already knew that The Rattlers and the Tall Boys would not play and also The Wild Ones pulled out later on. I was a bit disappointed about the Wild Ones. Their mini-LP on Earthworks is brilliant. Anyway, an American band called The Quakes was standing in and we were promised a special surprise act as well – so it all looked ok. The only setback was that I was the MC!

The first band was from Holland and called The Bang Bang Bazookas – honestly! They were a really good straight Rockabilly act with a very good-looking singer. However, I feel that they were a little too 'trad' for what really a crowd made up of 80% German Psychos. I liked 'em anyway. I shot off to grab some food while a Wallonian (South Belgian) band called The Jekylls came on. I didn't miss much by all accounts but I only heard their last song. Next up was the top French Psycho band Les Wampas, I had heard great things about this band but I was a little disappointed until towards the end of their set when they really turned it on and the vocalist gave it everything. A bit off-putting to hear everything sung in French but given some better songs this band could go places.

By now the promoter was getting worried because two bands hadn't turned up. The Quakes made it with thirty minutes to spare. These guys were great! A sort of Psychobilly Stray Cats – surely, they must make it to record soon! Then came the band that really started to get the crowd going – The Coffin Nails. This was the best I'd heard them play and a German promoter offered them a tour on the spot. People were saying that they were the new Meteors! They were followed by The Krewmen who are immensely popular in Germany. The crowd went mad during their set.

And then the best European band ever. Yes, Batmobile. Called in at the last moment to plug in the gap left by The Rattlers and the Tall Boys, Batmobile were better than both of them put together. You've guessed it – I'm a fan. I just loved Eric's Viking helmet. After them, The Meteors had it all to do and in all honesty for me they failed. A lot of people walked out during their set which was a bit like 'going through the motions'. It has to be said that they're in the middle of a large tour and maybe were a bit tired. They were better the last time I saw them at the Klub Foot.

We do it all again in six months' time. So far booked are Skitzo, Torment and the GuanaBatz as well as some German bands. Dig ya later, potato.

Captain Zorch.

With this review sent in by the boss of Nervous Records, I made a mistake, I did not include it in issue three of The Crazed. I was a Meteors fan and was chuffed to bits to have obtained an interview with P. Paul Fenech for issue two. I did not want to print any negative comments about bands in The Crazed especially The Meteors. What I should have done is contacted Roy or maybe edited that part of the review, but ridiculously I shelved it. Roy was a great, knowledgeable bloke and could have contributed some great articles. Fortunately, it didn't affect his attitude to me when I met him at the Klub Foot or rang him for updates on the bands he had on his label.

Boz Boorer and issue 3.

I had previously contacted Boz Boorer about a possible interview and then out of the blue received a letter from him. Boz had yet to join Morrissey and gain international recognition. In the early eighties Boz had been guitarist for The Polecats who had helped to bring Rockabilly back into the national charts with a great cover version of David Bowie's 'John I'm Only Dancin'' and their own song 'Rockabilly Guy' has become a classic. The Polecats had managed to gain the fame and recognition that many of the other bands featured in The Crazed never achieved. He wrote:

Dear Crazed.

You phoned me a while back about doing a interview and maybe a flexi. Well, what happened? I went on holiday, also did a compilation l.p. in Holland with seven Dutch bands who were really good. It's on Disky Records, I should send you a copy.

Also thinking of doing me own label with Stropper the D.J. First off would be a 'Tupelo Chainsex' l.p. a mad band from Hollywood and then maybe licensing some stuff. It's quite exciting.

Still managing Howlin' Wilf and The Vee-Jays, doing a new maxi single for Waterfront Records with a new line up.

Deltas are going to Holland for eight dates at the end of September, I don't think I'll survive.

Still a bit of writing here and there and home demos occasionally. The Caravans look as though they might be doing an l.p. and I'd like to get involved with that if I could and The Wigsville Spliffs.

Did some demos with the GuanaBatz in January but nothing came of it – it was a bit rushed.

I did me top ten.

> Shake 'em up Rock – Benny Cliff Trio
> Rock On the Moon – Jimmy Steward
> Boppin' to Grandfathers Clock – Sidney Jo Lewis
> Whoo I Man Whee – Hardrock Gunter
> Ride a White Swan – T. Rex
> Everybody's Body – George Hamilton IV
> Boots are Made for Walking – Tupelo Chainsex
> Chicken Walk – Hasil Adkins
> What's Inside a Girl? - The Cramps
> Oakie Boogie – Jack Guthrie
> I Got a Brand New Pair of Boots – Wildman Fisher

That's about it for now,

Boz Boorer

For some reason I never featured Boz's top ten records (although he listed eleven!) in The Crazed. The letter interestingly provides a glimpse of how productive Boz and the rockin' scene was during the eighties. An interview was promptly arranged to be undertaken at Boz's house in West Hampstead. So, on the 1st November 1987 I was on my way to interview Boz. I will never forget sitting on the train staring out of the window and thinking that I was about to meet Boz Boorer at his house, for someone so much into the scene it was almost a surreal moment. The Crazed was certainly providing me opportunities that most fans would not be able to get. Here was I, the lad who previously had the idea of starting a fanzine and sending off numerous letters to bands now on my way to spending the day with Boz. I will let the teenage me take over, from issue three:

It was a cold wet dreary Sunday morning when I set off to West Hampstead. The trains were disrupted due to engineering works on the line, so all the times of the trains were set back. Finally, I arrived in London, immediately after getting off the train I searched for a phone "Hello Boz" I said, "Uh, oh good where are you?" a very weary sounding Boz Boorer replied, "Boz can you tell me the names of the tube lines I have to get on". I later found out that this call had woken Boz up. "See you in twenty minutes then Boz", "Yeah, okay I'll meet you at the tube station". So, after I got off the tube, I waited outside the station for Boz, after a couple of minutes he arrived decked out in donkey jacket and cap and taking his dog out for a walk, he immediately looked over "Hello Paul, been waiting long?". So, with tape recorder in hand we ventured back to Boz's humble abode.

The interview wasn't conducted until about six hours later, in all that time Boz played me some of his demos, a live tape of The Caravans and The Deltas, some unreleased Polecats songs, some tracks off albums by an American band he's very enthusiastic about called Tupelo Chainsex, a demo by The Slingshots in fact loads of stuff. Also, a mate of his called Paul came round, and we then ventured off to an audio, cycle radio jumble, they picked up Jonny Bridgewood formerly of Fireball XL5 and The Sting-Rays along the way. Nobody bought anything apart from Boz who bought an amplifier with no insides for £25 and a rare flexi disc for £1 (as Boz collects rare records) and a mate of Jonny's bought a £45 cymbal and drumsticks. Boz tried to get a receipt off the stallholder as the amp was bought for Howlin' Wilf and The Vee Jays but to no avail.

So, after that we ventured back to Boz's place, Boz put the kettle on, his mate Paul left and Jonny and his mate stayed. Jonny playing his guitar that was round Boz's house and his mate started reading a music book very silently. Boz then came in with the tea: "Well, shall we do the interview now?" he asked. So, he went in the other room, and I got my tape recorder and the interview was finally conducted.

As most of you probably know, apart from playing in The Deltas, managing Howlin' Wilf, producing and playing on classic albums such as 'James Deans of the Dole Queue' Boz used to play for The Polecats who hit the charts around the same time as The Stray Cats, I asked Boz whatever happened to The Polecats? "Um, nothing really, it just fell apart. I left I joined The Shillelagh Sisters and they tried to get another guitarist in who was actually Andy who's now in Howlin' Wilf but that didn't work out and they went into managing and just sort of stopped playing and I just started playing with The Shillelagh's and they said you can't play in two bands and

I was getting paid for The Shillelagh's and I wasn't getting paid for The Polecats, I mean they done two gigs in a year so I left". Is there any chance The Polecats might reform? "I'll be up for it. It'll be a laugh but Tim doesn't get on with Phil anymore they broke up over the management thing and Tim doesn't want to do it, but he might when he gets really skint". I wondered looking back on it what was Boz's favourite moment with The Polecats? "It was all fun. It got a bit heavy towards the end they weren't using any of my ideas and I was just playing it was pointless. When it just started getting really popular and we started going down really well and people going mad at our gigs that was fun around '81 when we first got signed around that time". As Boz has produced so many rockin' bands since he left The Polecats, I wondered whether he had produced anything for the band? "I didn't use to take much interest in producing then, Tim and Phil had more of an idea what they wanted it to sound like, I like didn't really take much interest in it".

As recently Boz has produced more records than he's played on does he see himself more as a producer now than a performer? "I don't really take playing live seriously anymore; I play with The Deltas but that's just fun. I keep thinking I'd like to get another band together, but I don't know what I'd play, what sort of thing to do, maybe I might one day". Boz has written so many songs for various bands and artistes, when he writes I wondered does he write a certain song for a certain band? "Sometimes, The Wigsville Spliffs track High Class Power I sat in here just with a tape deck and guitar and just put down loads of ideas and just sent them the tape 'cos they were getting stuck for tracks, getting a bit stale writing wise and the Red Hot 'n' Blue thing 'Wait 'n' See' was just a track I had lying around for ages, I was going to give it to The Chevalier Brothers about a year before I gave it to Red Hot 'n' Blue, I suddenly thought I'd send it to Ashley (the bands guitarist) so I just sent him a cassette and said here Ashley I wrote a song for you and they did it and it was the title track of the album".

When did Boz first get involved with the production side of records? Boz points at Jonny: "That's with his lot Fireball XL5 it was Trisha the sax player out of The Shillelagh Sisters she said to me, oh, I was talking to Ray Frensham (who owned Northwood Records) up at one of the gigs and he was saying he wanted you to produce some band, so I thought that would be a laugh so we did it. It was the first thing I'd ever done so it was very rushed and inexperienced, and the band didn't have any bloody equipment, but it was a laugh and it went on from there really. I just did all the Northwood stuff". Boz is now even improving his production all the time as he's now working in a recording studio recording many different styles of music and using all the latest digitalized recording equipment.

Boz as I said previously has worked with many different bands, which has been his favourite band? "I suppose Howlin' Wilf because he's got such a brilliant voice. I really enjoy working with good singers any sort of music I just get into and sort of do but the Wilf thing's kind of special, I think that's why I got into the management side of them". So how did you originally get involved with them? "He came round my house to do a track on the Dance To It album and Wilf turned up with this other band and they said that our mates going to sing a song. I had that a couple of times during the week (as the album was recorded in Boz's house for one week) and it was a bit strenuous, and he just sat there, and they did their own songs then he started. I started laughing as he had such a great voice and then he got his own band together and he came in and did some demos and that didn't really get off the ground 'cos I don't think the band were charismatic enough, they didn't shine and then Tony who I had worked with, with The Lone Stars he phoned me up 'cos his harmonica player left and the band was like splitting up and he said, do you know any harmonica players, I want to get a bluesy bass thing together, I said there's Wilf who's got a great voice but I don't think he'll ever move out of Colchester. So I gave him his number and he phoned him up and he went to have a jam then they went busking and they came here and did a demo, then they did an album. They did the album here (recorded in Boz's house) and soon after that they started getting really busy and they asked me if I would manage them, so I did. Tony and Dot have now left the band so Howlin' Wilf and The Vee Jays have a new line up.

Is there any band that Boz would particularly like to work for? "Every band, not really, I never think of it like that really until the band approaches me or whatever, The Caravans maybe that would be fun (by the way did anyone see Caravans drummer Lee Barnett on Blind Date) that would be good, I'll do that". An album which featured Boz producing The Caravans was the excellent James Deans of the Dole Queue album, Boz explains his views about that album: "I thought it was great, I really liked it. I thought the bands were really good they didn't sound too samey either. I don't know how many it's sold, it should have been out a lot earlier than it was out, it came out six months to a year after it should have done, and it still did well". Does Boz ever worry that as he's written, played on, and produced so many songs that one day he'd have burnt himself out? "No, I go through patches of not being able to write songs just got no inspiration and then you can write ten in a day or something, the best songs are written sitting on the bog in three minutes". So how do you get to write a song is it just a sudden flash of inspiration? "Sometimes it's like a lyric or tune or a riff, there's different ways it comes about, sometimes it's two different songs and you put them together and you get a good one out of it".

A band that Boz has been closely linked with recently has been The Deltas, whom he plays for and also produced their Mad For It album, as well as writing most of the songs on it. How did Boz first get involved with The Deltas? "They phoned me up, Pat (the guitarist) had had an accident and he chopped the top bit of one of his fingers off at work and they wanted to go out and do some gigs, so they phoned me up and said do you want to play? and I said great 'cos I used to like The Deltas anyway, so we did a few gigs just doing the old stuff and then we'd get together every Christmas and do a handful of gigs". Then Boz heard an American band called Tupelo Chainsex whom he was thinking about: "Forming a band around and I might as well do it with The Deltas extend it, play them the Tupelo stuff see if they like it and then write some new songs, which we did". Then emerged The Deltas Mad For It album which Boz produced, wrote and played on, along with The Deltas.

For the future Boz hoped to form his own record company but due to too many hassles and lack of time he has it seems pretty doubtful it will ever get off the ground. So, apart from that for the future Boz says: "I want to have a baby and I want to clear all this mess out of this room and make it into two rooms so I can have an office here, (laughs) oh no that's not what you mean. I just take things as they come, more recording, more writing, maybe more playing, whatever". We then enter Boz's front room, Boz then gets a videocassette of all The Polecats promos and television guest spots and plays them for me, he sits there with a proud grin on his face looking at his past glory. After that I bid my farewells and leave Boz to probably write some more songs or whatever. Boz Boorer a name we certainly haven't heard the last of yet.

We certainly didn't hear the last of Boz as he later joined up with Morrissey and gained worldwide recognition as a prominent member of his band. The Polecats also reformed and played numerous gigs and recorded a new album for Vinyl Japan. Boz has remained active within the rockin' scene and his contributions would be too numerous to mention, Boz Boorer a one-man rockin' machine.

Skitzo.

From the calm of interviewing Boz Boorer I then set myself the task of interviewing Skitzo! They had released their classic debut album Skitzo Mania on Nervous Records and had become a regular fixture at the Klub Foot. The interview was to be conducted during the evening of the recording of Stomping at the Klub Foot Volume Five. The bands manager Oggie had arranged for me to be given a backstage pass for this prestigious night on 16th January 1988. So, armed yet again with my trusted tape recorder and a set of questions myself and a mate ventured up to Hammersmith. My mate had never been to the Klub Foot before and was in awe. When I met the band Oggie proceeded to give me the promised backstage pass which I proudly stuck onto my coat. We proceeded to follow the band into the venue. As it was a while before the venue opened to the public we decided to venture into Hammersmith, my mate was informed by the band that he may not be able to get back into the venue without paying for a ticket, so he decided to stay and hide in the toilets. We left whilst he locked himself into a cubicle. A little while later I was standing outside the Klub Foot with the band all sharing a bottle of Cider the band had bought. To everyone's surprise my mate appeared and explained that he been found and was told in no uncertain terms to unlock the door of the cubicle and get out. Fortunately, he had brought enough cash along to buy a ticket. Later that night when the band performed their set, I had the privilege of standing by the side of the stage with Oggie and their roadie Jerome who had brought raw Liver and chased everyone with it. It was a great moment for me to be up on stage (although in the wings) with them. How could I have ever thought in my wildest dreams when I was listening to Volume One in my bedroom that one day, I would be on stage for the recording of Volume Five. So here is the interview reproduced from issue three.

It was the night of the recording of Stomping at the Klub Foot volume 5 and a good time I thought to interview Skitzo! Skitzo should be known to most of you through their Skitzo Mania album and very successful and somewhat chaotic stage performances. The band has certainly in the last year built themselves up to being one of the best bands on the Psychobilly scene and their album was the bestselling record for Nervous Records last year. They've gone down really well in Europe especially Germany where their following is growing bigger all the time. The band consist of Phil who sings and screams for the band, Mac on guitar, Tony (Moses) on double bass and new drummer Strut who has introduced the full drum set within the line-up. The band was previously known as The Electros but decided to change to Skitzo and forget their earlier performances, it certainly paid off for the band as they've now played most of if not all the prestigious Psychobilly venues gaining even more recruits to the Skitzoid Dance Formation Team. They're even opening their own Psychobilly venue the Goo Goo Muck Club which as the advert for the club says is 'a weekly Psycho venue run by Psycho's for Psycho's'. The club is being run by Tony and Strut, they hope to feature many new Psychobilly bands who are finding difficulty in getting gigs in the rather restricting amount of venues for them to play in this country. Tony and Strut seem extremely enthusiastic about this venue when I talked to them about it and would like to hear from any Psychobilly bands who would like to play there. Could it emerge into the next Klub Foot?

Skitzo's album Skitzo Mania was received well when it was released and certainly paved the way for the band, proving to be an impressive debut album. The band though felt the production let it down a bit as Phil explains: "It was sad the outcome of it but now we appreciate the fact that it's all okay", "And we're still skint" comments Tony. "I tell you what I think had a lot to do with it" explains Mac: "They didn't let us be at the mixing that had a lot to do with it", "Good point" agrees Phil. Apart from the album Skitzo also had a video of an early Klub Foot appearance released on JettiSoundz, part of the soundtrack was also used on the Sick Sick Sick Klub Foot compilation album on ID Records. The band appeared to be a bit coy to comment about the video: "It was alright I suppose" Phil says, "No comment" Mac replies. I did find out that the band didn't have any say in the editing of it although it didn't really bother them as Mac says: "What's editing?", not being a video producer, I declined to explain, anyway I'm doing the interviewing. I wondered if the band were offered to do another video how they would go about it this time: "We'd all wear clean clothes" replies Mac, when the rest of the band asked Mac why he explains: "Well that's what they say on the telly isn't it these businessmen".

Nervous Records are negotiating with Skitzo to do another album due to the success of the Skitzo Mania album. When I contacted Roy Williams head of Nervous before the release of the album the enthusiasm, he showed for the band was extremely evident, he even thought the album was worthy of getting a place in the national charts. But unfortunately like most Psychobilly bands the band were virtually ignored by the music papers and so the album had to sell mostly through word of mouth. I begin to ask the band about how Nervous originally became interested in them when some classical music suddenly thunders through the Klub Foot pa. "What's that music?" jokes Mac. We then go back to the question as the music quietens down: "I think he was drunk at the time" says Mac explaining Roy Williams enthusiasm for the band. "He was he didn't know really what he was doing and then we had the contract" explains Phil, "and then when he was sober it was too late, we were signed" jokes Mac. "He didn't know he didn't care" someone jokingly says in the background. The band then explained their views about the music press which although is a regular topic of conversation in The Crazed interviews is always an important topic to cover especially in an interview situation as most of the bands haven't been interviewed before due to being ignored by the music press. Phil told me that this is the first proper interview(?) the band has done and remember this is an established band, it doesn't give a lot of hope to all the up-and-coming bands. Here's Skitzo's comments on the music press: "They can't accept it, can they" explains Mac commenting on the press attitude towards Psychobilly: "The thing is they don't know what's going on, like once The Meteors got a bit of coverage on the front page and that, but they don't know what's going on, that's why all they need is someone with a bit of brains to get them going, go to gigs" explains Strut. "Get them to do a write up about it not just us but all Psychobilly bands" says Mac. Strut: "The last Psycho write up I saw they slagged it off cos of the dancing". "They just don't understand" concludes Phil.

The Crazed issue 1.

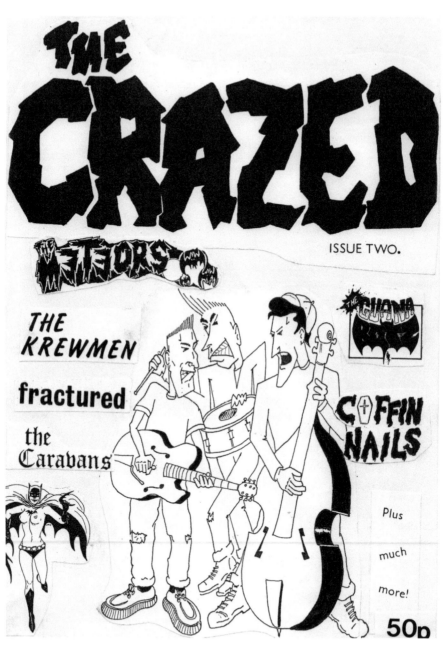

The Crazed issue 2.

The Crazed issue 3.

The Crazed issue 4.

Paul,

Happy drunken Christmas
from King Kurt

E'lo, namesake, Have
a jolly time over
The holidays! Paul

with
festive
beard   Rory
Happy Christmas
Maggot!

Watch out for us in January - we're off again

King Kurt Christmas card sent in the 80's to the author.

The Sting-Rays (courtesy of Richard Smith).

GuanaBatz ticket for The Angel Centre in Tonbridge.

Rod, Carl and myself posing in a photo me booth.

The Unknown's only ever gig in Chatham.

Some of the crowd who travelled up to see The Unknown Including Rod's brother Frank and his brother in law Charlie who was also the bands former drummer.

The Bloodstains featuring Dave Diamond.

Klub Foot flyer.

More Klub Foot flyers.

Myself and Marcus Heywood at the Klub Foot (courtesy of Marcus Heywood).

Torment (from authors collection).

Mark Carew from the Long Tall Texans (courtesy of Richard Smith).

Fractured at The Angel Centre, Tonbridge after my interview with them.

P Paul Fenech of The Meteors (courtesy of Richard Smith).

The Krewmen after my interview with them being photo bombed by GuanaBatz drummer Diddle.

Pip and Stuart from the GuanaBatz just after my interview with Stuart.

The Coffins Nails (from authors collection).

Flyer for the Wieze Psycho Festival.

Boz Boorer reading The Crazed.

Skitzo onstage at The Klub Foot for the recording of Stomping at The Klub Volume 5.

Oggie Skitzo's manager backstage at The Klub Foot.

Some of the crowd at The Klub Foot watching Skitzo.

A flyer for the Goo Goo Muck Club.

Restless (courtesy of Jeff Bayly).

Klub Foot ticket for a Meteors headliner.

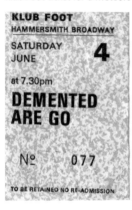

Klub Foot ticket for a Demented Are Go headliner.

A sketch drawn outside The Klub Foot by The Klingonz.

Shark Bait inside The Klub Foot after my interview with them.

Demented Are Go alongside fan who happened to walk upon my interview with them inside The Klub Foot toilets.

The Quakes by Camden Lock just before the line up split up.

The Lost Souls (from authors collection).

KLUB FOOT
The Boston, Junction Rd. N19

SUNDAY
25 SEPTEMBER

Camouflage presents

THE METEORS

No 453

TO *BE RETAINED*

Klub Foot ticket for The Boston Arms.

Town & Country Club
8-17 Highgate Road NW5

SUNDAY 11th SEPTEMBER 1988 Doors 3.30p.m.

Camouflage present

The Guana Batz

Admission £5.00 advance

N° 8 1 6

TO BE RETAINED

NO RE-ADMISSION

Ticket for the Psychobilly night at The Town and Country Club in 1988.

Woodie Taylor (courtesy of Richard Smith).

Glenn Daeche (courtesy of Richard Smith).

Red Hot Riot after my interview with them at Bedlam Psychobilly Festival, Northampton.

Soap and Tony from The Defiant Ones.

Jeff Bayly (courtesy of Jeff Bayly).

"How did we originally get together?" asks Mac, "He knocked on my door" explains Tony pointing to Mac, "Oh yeah and said you want to play bass and he says I can't play it and I said me I can't play guitar" explains Mac, "So we said perfect" jokes Tony. When I asked the band about what they were doing before they formed the band Tony answers: "Well I was in this band called the Sex Pistols and they sacked me". Somehow Strut ignores the question and answers my previous question: "Skitzo got together cos it was a cosmic happening, I had a vision one night I saw these four people get together and it was brilliant just cosmic". "You couldn't get any more cosmic than that" jokes Tony. Strut then summarises in two years' time: "We should be the biggest band going" on the Psychobilly scene? "Definitely!" he answers.

The band then explained how their unique cover version of the old Hank Williams classic Your Cheating Heart came about, Phil explains somewhat unbelievingly: "Well I can tell you that in one, it starts off slow because we used to play the record on a gramophone and the needle was slipping and Mac said let's do it slow then fasten it up. Right boys?" he asks. "No, I never said that!" shouts Mac, "I told a lie and they found me out" jokes Phil. Skitzo's manager Oggie then speaks: "You realise you're going to have to make your own words up" he jokes whilst trying to get some serious talk from the band. After his interjection the band then seriously answered the question there's no denying the wrath of a manager: "It's slow like really a piss take" explains Phil, "Yeah like Rock 'N' Roll beat at the beginning and Skitzo beat at the end, Psychobilly" says Mac. "We thought it would work better" concludes Phil.

The band have gone down really well aboard, they've become an extremely popular Psychobilly band in Germany. "We're pretty surprised we had a following like that" says Phil explaining the following they've gained there. "They're mental over there" continues Phil, "They're mental over here, but like you're restricted in places. like you've only got a certain amount of venues, but over there you can get them in every night. I mean you ask any band that's played over there, and they say there's more venues so there's obviously more people" concludes Phil.

Anybody wondering what Skitzo's previous alias The Electros

sounded like, well it was an infant sounding Skitzo. They had 'Doctor Death', and 'Psycho Baby' in their set plus an interesting early version of 'Going Skitzo' entitled 'Going Electro' plus a cover version of the old 'Blue Cats' classic 'Live Fast Die Young'. No recordings were ever released but after a line-up change, being that they changed drummers the band renamed themselves Skitzo and since then there's been no stopping them.

Going back to talking about Skitzo songs I wondered what the lyrics to 'Doctor Death' were about, which was a track off the Skitzo Mania album, Phil explains: "It's about a geezer whose car breaks down and he's stuck in the woods and then suddenly just like a horror film something jumps out and then the next thing he knows he's surrounded by a load of schizophrenics." Mac then takes up Skitzo's alternative version of Jackanory: "and then out of nowhere he's got somewhere to hide, and he sees this Tesco box behind the bushes, so he jumps in it, rolls inside a Sainsbury's bag and then...." that's enough. I don't know, questions like that always seemed to work in interviews in papers like New Musical Express, oh well. Tony then explains how a Skitzo song is written: "We all chip in but Phil writes all the words". The band then explain the influence behind their sound: "We started off as Psychobilly we didn't start off as a Rock and Roll band like all the others" says Tony. "We decided to be Psychobilly from the start" explains Mac "and I've got no Psychobilly records in my house" he continues, so why play Psychobilly then Mac: "Well otherwise I'll be influenced by them, that's why we've got our own sound" he answers.

The band are now looking forward to the release of their new album, will it be produced by Doc Stewart again? I ask "No" Mac says, "Produced by the geezer who writes The Crazed" but seriously lads! "We'll probably do it ourselves" Phil explains. There's also talk of a Skitzo compact disc being released by Nervous in the future. Also, in the future Tony explains his ambition: "I'd like to see myself in a fridge" why? "I've never seen myself in a fridge before" he answers. Mac them puts a label on Skitzo: "We're not Rockabilly and we're not Heavy Metal we're Psychobilly". The last question is asked, and Mac then explains: "I think the plan is now to go get drunk".

Skitzo then performed their slightly shambolic set for the recording of the live album with me observing from the side of the stage. I remember going backstage immediately after their set and seeing Strut slumped against a wall with a cloud of perspiration rising from him. Oggie later sent me a letter, which shows I must have taken up Mac's advice on getting drunk.

'Hi Paul, Hope you got home ok you old piss head. Here's the photo hope it's ok. It's all I have at the moment, so could you send it back please. Hope to see you on Sat'.

The photo sent was used for the article. Mac later left the band to be replaced by a guitarist called Pete who was a Klub Foot regular, I remember talking to him outside the Klub Foot before he joined the band. He brought a much heavier sound which is demonstrated on their next album 'Terminal Damage'. Many years later Phil's brother Rod joined the band on drums but very sadly is no longer with us. Skitzo were a great band and good fun to be around, even though not the most serious interviewees.

The Terminal Club.

Graham 'Smurf' Murphy who was guitarist for The Unknown for their one and only gig in Chatham had joined a new band called The Terminal Club who were not Psychobilly or Neo Rockabilly they were as in the band's description 'Red Hot Rockin' Blues'. The band were made up of members from other rockin' bands including another local band 'The Roanoke Rhythm Combo' who had released a single 'Swing It Little Katie' that had graced my collection. I spoke to the singer Neill Sanecki who agreed to provide me with a write up of the band for The Crazed.

The Terminal Club are a five-piece band from the Medway towns and North Kent. Each band member having an interest in early Blues Rockers, got together about one year ago and play in their own style a form of Rocking Rhythm and Blues. Influenced by the likes of Houndog Taylor, John Lee Hooker, Muddy Waters and Arthur 'Big Boy' Crudup.

The band have already played at venues in London such as Dingwalls, The Clarendon, The Crypt and at several venues in Kent such as The Stanley Ballrooms in Chatham, Club Musique in Maidstone and White Lion in Folkestone.

Future gigs are booked at The Sunset Strip in Chatham, Peggy Sues in Ramsgate, Bottoms Club in Folkestone, Town Hall in Chatham and a short tour of Belgium is being arranged for May.

Band consists of:
>Lead (and slide) guitar: Graham Murphy, formerly of The Roanoke Rhythm Combo.
>Lead guitar: Ashley Kingman, formerly of Red Hot 'n' Blue.
>Vocals and rhythm guitar: Neill Sanecki, formerly of The Roanoke Rhythm Combo.
>Drums: Ian Skoda, formerly of Thee Waltons.
>Double Bass: Tony Nihill: formerly of Nobby and The Balloon Pilots.

A few tracks were recorded a couple of weeks ago, produced by Mr. Boz Boorer and either a tape or 10" single will be available shortly......

I was at the gig at 'Peggy Sues' which was the main nightclub for over hormonal teens in Ramsgate during which Neill dedicated a song to me "This is for the magazine man". His article has provided an historically fascinating list of old venues that rockin' bands played during the eighties. I don't know whatever happened to The Terminal Club, I am not aware they released any recordings.

Get Smart.

Get Smart were an amazing band and in my humble opinion one of the best bands I saw at the Klub Foot. The band seemed to ooze coolness in both their sound and image. Roy Phillips the bands singer possessed a great presence on stage and owned a unique and cool voice. The band created an exciting rockin' sound, topped off with Jazz influenced Jimmy Fahy's drumming. I had first heard the band on the Nervous compilation album Zorch Factor One which featured the great 'It's Up to You'. Nervous also released their debut album, unoriginally entitled 'Get Smart'. The album was often on my turntable and still sounds as vital and fresh today as it did all those years ago. The following is taken from an interview with Roy at the Klub Foot and a list of written answers sent to me by the band's bass player Jonny Bowler, as the interview with Roy had to be cut short due to the times of the trains getting home.

One of the most exciting bands to come out of 1987 must surely have been Southampton quartet Get Smart. They released a really good debut album on Nervous which included many great rockin' tracks including an excellent cover of Buddy Holly's Baby Won't You Come Out Tonight. In my opinion it was one of the best rockin' albums released by Nervous and also showed that the more traditional sound certainly wasn't being swept aside by the Psychobilly invasion. The band create a fifties style slap bass rockin' sound with a bit of Swing and Jazz thrown in for good measure as well adding Modern Rockabilly to the mix. This comes out well in their live act with singer Roy Phillips entertaining the crowd in his own unique style, I mean this man got the Klub Foot wreckers wrecking to a track off Elvis's debut album, the track being Money Honey, which is no mean feat. So, we at The Crazed reckoned it was about time an interview with Get Smart was needed for The Crazed, so then here you are.....

First topic, the band's debut album, what did the band think about it? Jonny Bowler the band's bassist replies: "Well, I think we've all got mixed feelings about our album. I think we would have liked a more live feel to it then we got. The material we recorded in Southampton was recorded basically live then vocals/second guitar was added after. The tracks done in London however were recorded separately and I think this comes across you tend to lose a lot of the life in the music when you're not playing together. Also, I think it's very important for the band to have a say in the final mix as only the people who play the music know how they want it to sound and how it should sound. I think what you may lack in experience can be made up for enthusiasm". How did the band originally get the record deal with Nervous? Jonny replies: "A couple of years ago we did a demo tape in a local studio (six tracks, five original and one cover) and sent it to a few record companies and promotional agents. Nervous wrote back asking for more info and so after a few phone calls our first recorded track It's Up to You came out (off the demo) on Zorch Factor One. Roy Williams then came to see us play at the Klub Foot as so far, he hadn't seen us at all. After the gig we had a chat and made arrangements for an album. So, we signed for twenty tracks after a gig at the Clay Pidgeon, twelve of which went on our album the other eight for future compilation albums". So, is the deal with Nervous just a one off? Roy Phillips the band's vocalist answers: "It's a one off, I mean if there's more there's more, but we think of it as a one off".

So then, how did Get Smart originally get together? Jonny replies: "Everyone in the band had been friends before the band came together. Me and Rich played in a band called 'Git Fiddle and The Frenchies' a few years ago, and Roy was asked to sing, and the band became Get Smart, then Jimmy Fahy from the original Krewman line up was asked if he would like to takeover on drums and that's the line up on the album". But recently guitarist of the band Rich Caso has been playing partly in The Caravans, I wondered does this see a split emerging in the band? Jonny answers: "Since Rich had joined The Caravans there has been no real difference made in the band. Long before The Caravans asked Rich to play, the band had been playing together less and less, Roy has had to become a family man and so can't roam as freely as he used to, this added to the lack of venues to play means that things have been quite quiet lately. Though we all enjoy playing and it would take more than a few hold backs to put us off".

In the band's opinion, how different are Get Smart than your average rockin' band? Roy answers: "I think we're a laugh to watch so I've been told. We're tight, we like a more fifties sound than the new eighties sound. The majority of people I've spoken to, they prefer the more fifties side to it rather than the crash, bang, wallop stuff". So, what are Get Smart creating new? Jonny answers: "I think we've always tried to write songs which you can listen to. I don't think we are really creating anything new, maybe we're just thinking about music more than some other bands do. It's very easy to find one style of music or format for song writing and stick to it because of its success, but things soon become pretty dull if you don't alter your work. Even if something doesn't really work it doesn't hurt to have a go". How would you describe your music? "Our music has been described before as Jazzabilly, but I think basically Rock 'n' Roll is the only word necessary to describe this kind of music we play. People always like to have little pigeonholes for music and it's these categories that cause trouble". Jonny answers.

Talking of categories, I wondered what the band feel about playing in Psychobilly festivals abroad as the music they create can't be described as Psychobilly at all and neither can their image, Jonny takes up the point: "Playing Psychobilly festivals abroad is great fun even though we're not a Psychobilly band. The fans seem like a couple of years behind and they're really into it all. Hamburg with Skitzo was brilliant, I'm surprised we all got out! We receive a lot more mail from Europe than we do here and from all over Sweden, France, Germany Italy etc". What's been Get Smart's worst gig? "I don't think we've ever had like a really bad gig. The worst gigs we've played musically are normally the best laugh wise cos you can't play because you're drunk, so it doesn't really matter and the worst gigs to play crowd wise are your die hard 'Elvis patch/Stroller types where they spend all night dancing to some record that only the DJ knows who it is etc, I think they're basically a waste of time".

Song writing wise in the band Johnny explains: "Is done mainly by me and Rich getting together and playing until we come up with something that sounds good and then fit words to it, or sometimes words come first. Roy wrote most of our early stuff 'It's Up to You', 'Heavens Above', 'Ape Man' and then the music was added later. There isn't really any set pattern actually. I think we ought to think about writing some new songs". For the future the band are looking forward to playing at the recording of the new Klub Foot album which at the time Jonny explains is: "Inside info!", but you obviously all know about it now. Jonny hopes that Get Smart will have a new set by then: "It could be interesting" he says. I agree Jonny. I'll be there anyway or as it's now been recorded as the zine won't be out before the gig I was there, confusing, eh? then again, I never said it would be easy reading my interviews. Finally, the band have found it a bit of a restriction living in Southampton as Roy explains: "I mean Southampton's a place with a low profile anyway so of course we come from Southampton it's hard breaking out of it. It's a really hard town to break out of cos as we're not a London band or a closer band that's why we don't do so much". But let's not hope it's too much of a restriction for the band as what we've heard so far from them shows that they've got a lot more potential. So go out and see them live when you can or purchase their album on Nervous and then as the band would say..... Get Smart.

As mentioned, the band had so much potential that unfortunately remained unfulfilled as they regrettably didn't stay together long enough to record a follow up to their debut. Jonny later joined the GuanaBatz on drums and moved to America. Roy has recently remerged in a new band called The Black Kat Boppers and covered It's Up to You on one of their albums. A few unreleased live tracks from the recording of Stomping at The Klub Foot Volume 5 were released in 2014 on the Trophy Records box set Dragged from The Wreckage of The Klub Foot.

Restless.

Out of all the bands who might have achieved chart success and gain a large mainstream following were Restless. They had released two ground-breaking albums on Nervous Records which influenced many new and aspiring Rockabilly bands. Mark Harman's guitar playing set a very high standard and has become legendary. The band had the talent, the image and could write a decent song. Ice Cold a song from their debut album Why Don't You Just Rock remains a classic even to this day. For their third album the band had moved from Nervous and had signed to ABC Records who decided to release the much more polished and commercial sounding After Midnight which featured full colour photos of the band on the sleeve and even included a glossy colour poster featuring close up portrait photos of the band, which were very similar to photo shoots in teenage pop magazines like Smash Hits. The album still maintained a rockin' influence but would not have sounded out of place on daytime radio. I managed to secure an interview with Restless on 10th October 1987 at the Klub Foot and would be issued a backstage pass as the interview would be undertaken in their dressing room. So, with my backstage pass stuck onto my coat (it was a cool coat my Dad used to wear, it was vintage before the term vintage existed) I met the band and conducted what I felt was a very productive and interesting interview.

A Restless interview at the Klub Foot. After waiting awhile inside the venue whilst the band went through a sound check, the trio, myself and manager and producer of the band Pete Gage plus a couple of students doing a Restless topic for their homework (ie what are Restless' perversions type questions) went into the bands dressing room with our backstage passes stuck onto our coats to make sure no Klub Foot bouncer threw us out and the Restless interview with The Crazed was conducted.

Restless are probably the most commercially viable band on the scene, who don't really fall into the Rockabilly tag that most people like to stick them with. I wondered if the band do find it a restriction being labelled a Rockabilly band as the music they are making now can't really be described as Rockabilly? Mark Harman the bands singer and guitarist answers: "Yes, you're right actually by saying that we can't be labelled as Rockabilly, I mean what can nowadays really. I don't think there's such a thing as a true Rockabilly band anymore. So, it restricts us insomuch as big record companies or TV or anybody wouldn't want to touch anything to do with Rockabilly, cos they don't think it's commercially viable so it's a bit of a bind, but still good fun that's why we do it". So, you don't mind being classed as a Rockabilly band? "Yeah, we do but there's nothing we can do about it really, apart from tell people. Obviously, we don't have to tell people like you that it's not Rockabilly and most of our fans would know that anyway, so it's up to them to tell the people really, not really the music papers so much". Do you feel annoyed though that the music papers virtually ignore the band as they class Restless as a Rockabilly band, which isn't too favourable with the music press at the moment? Mark takes up the question:, "Yeah, I do feel annoyed about that but at the end of the day it matters to a certain extent, because we're trying to become very popular, and I suppose we need the music papers as a stepping stone. But it would be nice to be able to blow them out at a later date". Ben Cooper the bands drummer then explains why he believes the music press ignores Restless: "I don't think it's trendy. I mean it's alright for other types of bands, very famous people like get their influences from the sixties and seventies but because we've gone ten years before that, I mean it's like we've got the plague or something as we've got double bass and quiffs and so that's why they ignore us. If they came to a gig, they'd realise what's going on. I mean we don't go up there and play very quietly or anything, I mean most people leave our gigs with ringing ears, so I think they've just got to come and see us and then they'd realise. But as long as they think that we're not trendy they'll slag us off. I mean we can compete with any band doing any sort of music. So, I challenge them to come along to a gig and then slag us off". Do you think Rockabilly will ever come back in vogue again? Ben answers: "I don't know I think bands might come in, I think the odd band might breakthrough, but it will have to be someone like us".

With the release of their After Midnight album on ABC Records came a change of sound for the band. This third album was a lot more commercial sounding than the previous albums which were released on Nervous. How did a lot of the earlier fans of the band react to the change of sound on that album? Mark answers: "Well, a lot of them didn't like it, a lot of the new people did. It's like there's been a crossover, we lost some, but we gained some, so it didn't really affect us that much. There's been a lot of bad feeling about it because people didn't understand what we were trying to achieve, but that's the way it goes when you experiment and try and make it better for yourselves, that's what happens". I presume that it was trying to make Restless a more chart orientated band: "That was the idea was to achieve that but not sell out which we didn't do, a lot of people thought that we did but all we did was improvise on what we had in the first place which were good songs".

So, as the band have gone through as what they describe as the 'crossover' in their music, what do they now think of their first album Why Don't You Just Rock? which is Nervous Records biggest selling album, and which influenced a whole new breed of rockin' bands, Mark answers: "We still do some from the first album, It was very cheap, it brings back a lot of memories, it was a good time really, did it very quickly. When we listen to it I don't know what I think, I think what I was thinking then, which was that this is the beginning and we're going to be very rich megastar's within the year, and here I am seven years later still saying, it's a good album". Why did the band re-record 'Ice Cold' and release it as a single five years after it had originally appeared on their debut album? Mark replies: "Pete our manager was experimenting with it onstage it always goes down really well, we thought we'd do a better version or at least spend more money on this one that's why we did it". Do you think the re-recording came out well? "Yeah, I thought it came out well. I still like the first one, I never realised the first one was so much faster than the second one. I think they're both good really". To be a bit trivial what is your favourite Restless song? Mark answers: "I dunno really, I think if I've got a personal favourite is 'Vanish Without a Trace', I like that one probably because I didn't write it it's one of Ben's". Mark then turns to Ben and asks: "What's your favourite Ben?", "My favourite of yours is 'Trouble Rides a Fast Horse'" replies Ben. "Is it?" Mark says curiously, he then turns to Jeff Bayly the bands double bass player who's remained rather silent throughout the interview and asks which is his favourite Restless track "I was going to say that n' all, I like that one" he says agreeing with Ben.

The band were previously a four piece with the inclusion of Mick Malone on rhythm guitar. I inquire as to why he's left the band, Mark answers: "Um, I don't really know I haven't worked that one out yet. Pete, do you know why he left the band?". Pete Gage then takes up the answer: "Basically the problem Micky also is very keen on the Jazz influenced bands Swing Out Sister etc, and he's had a hankering to make that sort of music for some length of time. So, finally because his heart wasn't totally into Restless' music, he felt the best thing to do was to leave. We're all still best of mates and I'm actually trying to introduce him to a lot of people in that circle who he doesn't know. So that's really what it came down to it was a bit of a surprise because he talked about it for a long time, but we'd never thought he would actually get round to doing it cos Restless like just having fun with their music and found it a little strange that Micky wanted to take things a little more seriously, but that was his decision. The reaction has been a lot stronger since it's gone back to the three piece so Micky's actually done us a huge favour". So, will the band stay a three piece now? "Most certainly, yeah" Pete answers. So why did the band feel the need to get a second guitarist in the line-up? Mark answers: "Because we thought the sound was a little bit empty because Ben was standing up, he wasn't using the bass drum or anything. I had to work very hard, because I had to sing and I couldn't move at the same time, so Ben had to do that job as well. It was a bit silly really, so we thought we'd just get another man in just to make it look better really and fortunately it sounded a lot better as well. The sound was a lot fuller of course and then we could be a bit more daring with our song writing, 'cos he could handle a lot of the guitar work while I was doing something else, it just added another dimension to it all".

Keeping on the subject of previous band members, I ask Mark why Paul Harman the bands original double bass player left the band: "It's the age-old story of a woman, he sort of wanted to spend a lot more time with his girlfriend and it was his decision really. He didn't have any time left for the band and so decided it would be best if he left 'cos he was holding us back somewhat and he left and got married and got a couple of kids, house, carpet slippers, he's happy". How did you get Paul's replacement Jeff into the band? Mark answers: "We've always been friends, sort of live in a very small circle out in the sticks in Sudbury Suffolk and Jeff was an old friend, not school friend so much as a workmate, and we used to hang about together all the time. He took up double bass I think as Restless were already going, had been going for a few years even, it was just a natural thing to do was to get him in as soon as Paul left and fortunately it went well". Mark appeared in the Dave Phillips Hot Rod Gang on the Dave Phillips 'Wild Youth' album which included 'Tainted Love' which got in the lower regions of the national chart. I ask Mark why he left the Hot Rod Gang? "I didn't join them actually, I just did some session work for him, that's all I did I made an album with him that's it, then I couldn't stand him any longer". So, was it a personal reason?" No, I was with Restless at the time".

The follow up album to 'After Midnight' was the Live and Kicking album on ABC records. Are the band pleased with that album? Mark replies: "Yeah, I think it's better than the first Klub Foot album, it's pretty well done a lot better. I don't know about the cover, have you seen the cover yet? the photo on the backs a bit dodgy as well". Do you think it's a good example of a Restless gig? "Not really 'cos you have to be there. We're at our best when we play live, all the bands that are around even the GuanaBatz and that know we can top them when it comes to live music, maybe a lot of them aren't too mad about our records, but they still come and see us live because they know that we can really cut it. But the live albums good in so much it's a good sound and the people are cheering and everything, but you needed to see what was going on. Were you there that night by any chance? that was a good one, that was one of our better ones here". Do you find it harder playing gigs out of London? Mark replies: "I suppose yeah because we built up in London now after a couple of years and that so we're alright. If we go back to places and build up the audiences it's much better to do that, it's very difficult. We're building up Scotland at the moment and that's going along nicely. I'm actually getting well into university things at the moment cos they're going down down so well". The band's best reputation is at the Klub Foot as Mark explains: "We get more people here than anywhere I suppose, some Klub Foot's are absolutely brilliant others aren't so hot for some reason".

Apart from the release of the live album JettiSoundz Video also released a live video of the band, Mark explains his views on the tape: "There's one thing I've got to say about that, don't buy it. They released it without telling us, we never even saw it, seen it since and think it's pretty diabolical. If you're going to print something, then tell the fans not to buy it". Pete Gage then explains how annoyed the band are about the video, the band didn't see the final edited version of the film before it was released: "The minimum I have heard people pay is eighteen pounds and for that I think is absolutely terrible" he says.

If the band had to describe their music, how would they describe it? "Brilliant" Ben answers. Apart from that label obviously, "Good, just good music good Rock 'n'' Roll music. People can enjoy it you know" Mark replies. So where would you like to see it put in a record shop, under the Rockabilly section or the Rock and Pop section? "Heavy" Pete jokes. Mark takes up the answer: "That's a bit heavy yeah, the rock and pop section I think, but that's asking a bit too much really". Ben then answers: "I don't know it's just music like anything else, it's just a different sort. I mean just put it in the section with everything else I suppose". In issue two of this zine (plug plug) Fractured were speaking out about the Restless tag which certain people like to bestow on them, I wondered what Restless thought of hearing about bands who are said to be influenced by them? Mark answers: "I don't think they should be compared with us, it would be nice to know that they've got a lot of respect for us, if they sort of not rip us off but follow us in our footsteps that's a compliment for us. I think it's a good thing really. I don't think anybody can be compared with us, not meaning to sound conceited because we're so different, we're not like any other rockin' band really. We're not offended by it; I can understand it as a compliment in a way because we've been around a lot longer than they have and obviously if we're being compared there must be some similarities and if there are it's because they've copied us and not we've copied them".

So, finally what is Restless' main ambition? "Just to be very successful" Mark replies "And to be content with what we do, that's all we want to be successful. Obviously, that would be anybody's ambition surely, make lots of dosh". So, any further comments you

159

would like to say before the interviews finished? Ben says: "We're the best rockin' band on the circuit". There's a slight silence, after thinking about Ben's comment Mark replies: "It's not really for us to say when you think about it". "Well, I don't know it's a free country" Ben replies. I then leave the band in their dressing room to ponder over their last comment. The Klub Foot doors then open and in pours everybody, a lot of whom rush over to the T shirt store. Some Restless t shirts are sold, a Restless poster is also for sale. The band are unfortunately stuck in a rut, they want to broaden their audiences and popularity but they still get classed as being a Rockabilly band although they feel that the music they are now creating doesn't so easily fall into that category and deserves to be heard by a large audience, whether the band will succeed remains to be seen. So for the time being the band will have to be content with building up the name of Restless through gigging around the country and Europe.

Restless never achieved the national prominence that they wanted. Ben and Jeff later left the band (to both later re-join) and Mark Harman continued to release Restless albums, which continuously showed the band maturing. The respect and admiration for Restless has remained constant throughout the years. The band even played at Robert Plant's son's wedding with the legendary Led Zeppelin singer joining them on stage. If any band within the scene was going to break it, it would have been Restless, but the music scene was fickle, and trends moved on rather fast during the heady days of the eighties. Tastes could be just as fickle even at the Klub Foot, as during the night that I conducted the Restless interview I was standing within the venue with my Restless backstage pass still stuck onto my coat, which gained the attention of three Psychobilly's within the crowd, who must have assumed I was part of the Restless crew, I started getting dagger looks. I was also holding a bag protecting my cassette recorder which now included the newly recorded Restless interview. The looks continued, balancing the situation in my mind, I made a hasty retreat, there was only one of me and three of them, I certainly didn't feel like answering for the After Midnight album and losing my cassette of the interview! What days they were, when the progression and sound of a band seemed so important in our lives and if not favourable could lead to a kicking.

Torment questions.

Growing up I always enjoyed reading magazines like Smash Hits and Look In which often featured lists of trivia that bands often answered. I always found this interesting as it often gave insights into bands which more traditional interviews couldn't. I wanted to take this same approach with a band who had previously been featured within The Crazed. Torment seemed to be a good choice, as I was already in communication with drummer Kevin Haynes who was still providing me with excellent designs for my covers. So, a list of not so serious questions was sent, which fortunately each band member agreed to answer. Here are the results:

SIMON BRAND: VOCALS/GUITAR

FULL NAME: Simon John Brand.

DATE OF BIRTH: 12.01.65.

WHAT WAS YOUR SCHOOL REPORT LIKE: I was always on report, I failed five O Levels and gained three C.S.E.'s.

PREVIOUS BANDS: Firebirds, Frenzy, Jumpin' Jacks, Torment.

HOBBIES: Collecting photos, tickets, posters or anything of Torment, I have five scrap books full.

BEST GIG: Hamburg 1986, Nov.

MOST EMBARRASSING MOMENT: My Mother-in-Law giving me a packet of Durex on my girlfriends third or fourth date with me.

FAVE FOOD: Chips.

FAVOURITE BANDS: Sex Pistols, Demented Are Go, Tall Boys, Iggy Pop, B.B. King.

FAVE COUNTRY: Northern Europe.

AMBITION: To have two kids.

FAVOURITE TORMENT SONG: Con-scription Plan, Pass it On.

FAVE T.V. SHOW: Moonlighting and Cheers.

MOST FRIGHTENING MOMENT: Grizzly wanting to kick my teeth up my nose because someone told him I said his mixing was crap at the Klub Foot. But we're best of mates now.

WHAT WOULD YOU BE DOING IF YOU WEREN'T IN TORMENT: I would be in another Psycho band, playing guitar.

HIGHPOINT OF CAREER (SO FAR): Touring Germany and our 12" single.

SIMON CROWFOOT: BASS

FULL NAME: Simon 'Gorbachev' Crowfoot of the Sioux tribe.

DATE OF BIRTH: 15.6.1863

HIGHPOINT OF SCHOOL CAREER: Being unchained after the big bang.

PREVIOUS BANDS: Demented Are Go, Swamp Toads and Cultic Heads.

WHY DID YOU LEAVE DEMENTED ARE GO: Because Torment offered more opportunities.

WORST GIG: Switzerland, Zug in May '87.

MOST EMBARRASSING MOMENT: Playing stand in for The Firebirds, March 1986.

FAVE DRINK: Lager and Pils.

FAVOURITE RECORD: Take 5, Dave Brubeck.

FAVOURITE BANDS: Most Psycho bands with slap bass players.

FAVOURITE TORMENT SONG: Con-scription Plan.

FAVOURITE ACTOR/ACTRESS: Lauren Hutton and Angie Dickinson, both of these chicks are 'sex on a stick' (official Torment lingo).

WHAT WAS THE LAST RECORD YOU BOUGHT: Bert Weedon's 'Play in a day' extended Psycho mix.

WHAT WOULD YOU BE DOING IF YOU WEREN'T IN TORMENT: Be a tax exile in Outer Mongolia.

HIGHPOINT OF CAREER (SO FAR): Playing abroad and cutting records.

KEVIN HAYNES: DRUMS

FULL NAME: Kevin' Wookey' 'Let's make another record' Haynes.

DATE OF BIRTH: 22.5.64.

WHAT WAS YOUR SCHOOL REPORT LIKE: Well, I was a perfect student, I got straight A's in everything? Well, I was very close to Miss 'Saucy' Hill the Geography teacher.

PREVIOUS BANDS: Joey and The Gossamers, Joint Jumpers, Wild Range Hepcats.

WHEN DID YOU FIRST START PLAYING DRUMS: When I was 3½ my Mum and Dad bought me a twelve-piece Premier drum kit. One bang and I was addicted.

WHERE WOULD YOU MOST LIKE TO PLAY: In Psychobilly terms

we've played most of the best venues, but it would be good to play at any of the big London venues Odeon, Palais.

MOST EMBARRASSING MOMENT: Going to see Si Crowfoot play stand in for The Firebirds.

FAVE FOOD: Anything but German food!

FAVOURITE BANDS: I like the Texans, Skitzo, Get Smart, Highliners, plus all bands I do record covers for, but my favourite band is -: The Cramps WoW!

WHICH BAND (APART FROM TORMENT) WOULD YOU MOST LIKE TO DRUM FOR: Cor that's a hard one! The Bangles, I think it would be quite good in the dressing room!

FAVOURITE TORMENT SONG: Uncle Sam goes down well, The Last Time is pretty good although some other Psycho band now do it. But the new songs for the new album are better.

WHY DO TORMENT WEAR DARK GLASSES: Well in a previous life Si Brand was a killer Rabbit! So now he has pink eyes, so the glasses protects his eyes from the press, myself and Si Crowfoot wear our glasses in sympathy!

FAVE T.V. SHOW: Brush Strokes, Bilko, Hogans Heroes.

WOULD YOU LIKE TO APPEAR ON TOP OF THE POPS: Of course, we would! I can't wait to meet Bruno Brookes!

HIGHPOINT OF CAREER (SO FAR): Being billed on the same poster as Batmobile! I think the Belgium Psycho Festival in Dendermonde where we got mobbed in the town square?

So, there you are! Information and bits of trivia you would never have known about Torment. This unfortunately was the one and only time I used this format, which is a shame as I think it was a bit of fun. How else would you have learnt what the band were watching on T.V. or what their favourite food was or that Simon Crowfoot was born in 1863!!

Long Tall Texans top ten.

Mark Denman from The Long Tall Texans provided me with the bands favourite top ten records, which by now had become a regular feature of The Crazed.

Mark Denman: Guitar

1. Happy Home – The Screaming Blue Messiahs.
2. I Didn't Know I Loved You 'Til I Saw You Rock 'N' Roll- Gary Glitter.
3. I'm So Bored With.The U.S.A.-The Clash.
4. She Does It Right- Dr Feelgood
5. The Crawl- The Fabulous Thunderbirds.
6. Maniac- The Meteors.
7. Gear Jammer- George Thorogood and The Destroyers.
8. Just A Feeling- Bad Manners.
9. Stay Clean – Motorhead.
10. The Stumble- Freddie King

Mark Carew: Slap Bass and Vocals.

1. Come Back My Love- Darts.
2. Jealous Love- Alvin Stardust.
3. Half Hearted Love- Mac Curtis
4. Time Warp- Rocky Horror Show.
5. My Daddy Is A Vampire- The Meteors.
6. Clockwork Toy- Frenzy.
7. Longest Time- Billy Joel.
8. My Girl- Madness.
9. Silly Thing- The Sex Pistols.
10. My Babe- Little Walter.

Theo: Drums.

1. Ever Fallen in Love- Buzzcocks.
2. The Crazed- The Meteors.
3. Can't Hurry Love- Diana Ross.
4. Only Want to Be With You -The Tourists.
5. Stand Down Margaret- The Beat.
6. The Prisoner- The Clash.
7. Hersham Boys- Sham 69.
8. Red Red Wine- UB40.
9. Frenzy- Frenzy.
10. White Man in Hammersmith Palais- The Clash.

I cobbled together an introduction for issue three.

Hello again,

Well, here it is then, the third issue of The Crazed. Hope you all reckon it's alright. Due to the response we received you preferred the style of the interviews introduced in issue two as opposed to the style featured in issue one, so we've continued the style with this issue. Thanks to everyone who has been reading The Crazed since the beginning and welcome to anyone reading The Crazed for the first time.

Unfortunately, since the last issue popular rockin' trio Wigsville Spliffs have split up due to many reasons although they haven't totally ruled out reforming it does seem unlikely as Mike Lister the bands bassist now works on a night shift. It's a shame as they seemed to have a lot of potential and who could ever forget the bands classic 'Al Capone', a band who will be missed.

Anyway, I hope you enjoy this issue.

Cheers,

WATCH OUT FOR A NEW PSYCHOBILLY BAND CALLED THE KLINGONZ!!!!!

Reader's letters.

The reader's section had shrunk to half a page and featured edited versions of some of the mail I had received.

I received issue two of The Crazed the other day and was stirred to write to you. The mag was summed up in one word, Brilliant! I prefer the layout and style of no. two as well as the size and well worth (I think) 10p extra I thought the Batz interview came across well as did The Meteors one. How about an interview with Restless in the near future?
Letter sent in by Julian Temple, Thorpe St, Andrew, Norwich.

Just had to write to say how great The Crazed is, real informative and in-depth interviews at last. Ginger Meadham's latest band The Highliners must surely go far, what with their catchy songs, great stage image and TV appearances to boot, how can they fail?
Letter sent in by Craig Gardner Carlisle Cumbria.

This is a letter complaining to all Rockabilly and Psychobilly bands, what happened to Scotland? Bands that have been here seem to enjoy themselves, don't get me wrong travelling to England is great but we just can't afford it, so how about coming up to Scotland for once. Letter sent in by Steff (Cha), Baz, Tally, Dates-Denny, Stu, Aldo, Braco, Ray, Fish- Kilsyth, Scotland.

I am glad to see a magazine aimed at this particular music. Coming from the North East I don't get to see many bands as hardly any travel up here, which is a shame as there is a strong following of both Rockabilly and Psychobilly music. Letter sent in by Marsh, New Hartley, near Newcastle.

This issue was another one I was pleased with, although I don't think it was quite as good as issue two, I feel that the interviews came over well and hopefully displayed an insight into the bands and gave a personality and voice to the characters behind the music. But, looking back I can recognise three mistakes I made. The first was not featuring the gig review Captain Zorch (Roy Williams) sent me, the second was scaling back the reader's page and the third was having no interest in selling advertising space. But the teenage me just wanted to keep moving forward with the fanzine, meeting more bands and interviewing them. The Crazed was being read and I was on a roll.

Issue 4.

I started preparing for what would become the final issue of The Crazed. The Klub Foot was to close and would hold a farewell weekend of great gigs including Demented Are Go and GuanaBatz. I managed to arrange a couple of interviews during this, including an interview with the now legendary Demented Are Go. I did not realise at the time the impact the closure of that legendary venue would have on me, The Crazed and the Psychobilly scene within the United Kingdom.

Shark Bait.

Shark Bait were a band who it could be said were in the right place at the wrong time. They were a Dublin based Psychobilly band who played a blistering set during the night of the recording of 'Stomping at The Klub Foot Volume Five. Their contribution was certainly one of the highlights to a slightly underwhelming album. The band had started to become recognised during the period that the Klub Foot was preparing to close which would cause the scene to shrink within the United Kingdom including London. The band had a great blueprint for Psychobilly featuring a fast and furious sound with the addition of Dave Finnegan's energetic vocals. I met the band at the Klub Foot on their last ever performance there on 25th June 1988. I managed to talk to Dave Finnegan, guitarist Fergal Heapes and their manager Ritchie. The band were looking very optimistically towards the future and were looking forward to recording their debut album.

One of the most promising Psychobilly bands to emerge recently has been Shark Bait. They had two really good tracks included on the ABC Records series of compilation albums Stomping at The Klub Foot, the band were featured on volume five, taken from an exciting power charged set they performed there. Those two tracks and various successful performances at various gigs that the band have played soon helped the band to gain themselves an ever growing following. The band really established themselves well at the Klub Foot and it soon became common to see a quiffed Psychobilly walking around with a Shark Bait t-shirt on.

Lead singer Dave explains how Shark Bait have established themselves: "We've got a big following over here since we started playing last September with the Batz, then we done the Klub Foot album. We've had fan mail, which is pretty good, we've had letters since we've been on the Klub Foot album". Were the band pleased with the tracks featured on the Klub Foot album? Dave: "We were told we were the best band on the album, didn't think much of the album it was probably the worst Klub Foot album. We were pleased with the two tracks on it". Will your new material be similar to those two tracks? Dave: "Yeah, we have a live feeling about it 'cos people come to see us 'cos of our wildness on the stage, so we're going to try and make the album more wild". Would Shark Bait describe themselves as Psychobilly? Fergal the bands guitarist answers: "We're not going to say we're not 'cos everybody says that". Dave: "We're not going to say we're a pop band we're a Psychobilly band. What's the use about lying about it?". Fergal: "I'm proud of it". Dave: "When we started off two years ago, we were a Rockabilly Psycho band but now since we've got the new drummer we're really as you've heard on the Klub Foot album it's really heavy stuff which is what we're all into, it's really wild". So, what bands do the band listen to? Dave: "Batz, Demented Are Go, Stray Cats we listen to all the bands we play with, that's what we're into. We were into that when we started the band, so we still listen to it, like we still go out and buy other bands albums, still listen to old Rockabilly numbers like Johnny Burnette, Gene Vincent, listen to it all. The best band we've played with is Batmobile I think they are excellent; they were brilliant they were really good. Another band I would like to play with is Restless they are probably the best musicians in Psychobilly".

Observing Shark Baits influences would the band have been a Rockabilly band if it wasn't for the emergence of Psychobilly? Dave: "We probably would". Fergal: "R 'n' B or Rockabilly". Dave: "Like everyone has their own mixture, we wouldn't just do straight fifties Rockabilly, it's just not in you know". Fergal: "It would have been something like The Stray Cats sound I suppose". So, are The Stray Cats what first got you into the music? Fergal: "I got heavily into them; I was mad into Setzer". Dave: "They bought the hairstyles, I think they bought the big quiffs to Psychobilly like Fenech was supposed to start Psychobilly, Setzer bought the quiffs and all the image". So how did Shark Bait originally get together? Fergal: "Dave was in another band". Dave: "I was in another Psychobilly band, and we broke up, and I knew the bass player and we just knew Fergal and we asked him to join and come along he brought a drummer with him". Fergal: "That was in October 85". Dave: "Since then there's been a bit of a change, we've got a new drummer". Fergal: "We've gone through three managers, they all left us financially broke".

The band are hoping to release an album which they are negotiating about at the moment. The band explained how they are planning their albums, Dave: "Some bands tend to make an album great Psychobilly then they drop down on their second album, we'd like to keep up good rockin' albums so we wouldn't be boring, like wouldn't change the direction. If we did it would still be listenable, everybody would still be into it, good Psycho". Fergal: "All you can do is hope you play better on your next album, better producer or whatever". Dave: "Psychobilly's the main music that's why we're a Psychobilly band. We're just a Psychobilly band that's what we are. We've no plans to change into any other music". So, finally what have the band got planned for the future? Dave: "Europe hopefully and a British tour". he then turns to Ritchie the bands manager who says: "Not Europe until we get the record deal". Dave: "Yeah but that's what we've got planned for the future". Ritchie: "Oh yeah absolutely, think of all those girls in Europe". Dave: "We've been trying to get on a few supports to Europe. Just get a record out, so when the record goes to Europe everyone knows what we sound like, you want to have a record out to see what they think". Shark Bait are a band on the Psychobilly scene who it seems are going to go far. Definitely a band to check out live.

Shark Bait never got to release their anticipated debut album at the time as they later split up. In 1989 Dave Finnegan released some Shark Bait songs on Link Records for a band he got together called 'Scared Stiff', the album didn't have the impact that a Shark Bait release would have had, even though it featured a studio version of Johnny Cynic a song which was one of the highlights of the Klub Foot album. The band did eventually record an album called 'One More Bite' many years later in 2012 through meeting up on Facebook. Dave Finnegan did find some fame in 1991 by appearing in the film 'The Commitments'.

Demented Are Go.

Demented Are Go were also playing the same night as Shark Bait, so it seemed a good opportunity to interview them. The band had released an amazing album 'In Sickness and In Health' on ID Records, along with a single 'Holy Hack Jack' both records entered the independent charts. The band introduced their own unique sound and outrageous image to the scene. No one had sounded like singer Mark Phillips before. They did not sound like they were trying to copy anybody else; it was their own interpretation of a mixture of styles but with that essential rockin' sound. Their song writing was also strong even though most of the lyrics were quite risqué. The album was so good a friend of mine who was more Teddy Boy than Psychobilly borrowed it, unbeknownst to me he listened to it whilst he was styling his quiff and using copious amounts of hairspray which unfortunately embedded itself into the grooves of the vinyl, as his record player was placed behind him, the album came back with added crackling! much to my dismay. It took a matter of minutes before I was buying another copy from my local Our Price. Throughout the years the band has built up quite a reputation, especially Mark Phillips whose sometimes erratic behaviour is well documented within Nick Kemp's brilliant biography of the band Kicked Out of Hell. But meeting them on the night of their last performance at the Klub Foot I found the band approachable, amicable, and agreeable for an interview. Ant Thomas and Mark Phillips were the two members of the band who stayed for the duration of the interview with new bass player Graeme Grant making an eccentric appearance. The band were about to release their second album 'Kicked Out of Hell' which also featured new guitarist Lex Luther bringing a heavier sound. The interview started off being conducted in the bar area of the Klub Foot but due to the p.a. being so loud it became impossible to hear the band, so it was decided to find somewhere quieter, and a decision was made to continue the interview in the Klub Foot toilets which provided great acoustics and had no loud music drowning out our voices (I recall David Bowie's Let's Dance blasting out the p a). Even though the venue was not yet open a Psychobilly fan with a large 'Demented Are Go' logo on the back of his leather jacket came into the toilets, must have been a shock to have seen both Mark Phillips and Ant Thomas in there being interviewed by me! I saw a photo opportunity and asked him to stand in between Mark and Ant with the logo on his jacket facing the camera, he posed whilst the drummer and singer put their arms on his shoulders and then sharply left. I sometimes wonder what he must have told his mates! Is it a story to brag about, possibly if it was anywhere else but the toilets.

Demented Are Go Cardiff's finest, are certainly one of the most original bands on the scene, with their own unique sound. With many successful supports at Psychobilly gigs around Europe they soon rose to becoming a headlining band, with their crazy and sometimes manic stage act. The band also released a successful album on ID records which was called In Sickness and In Health in 1986 an essential purchase to any Psychobilly record collection. The album got to number nine in the independent charts and the single Holy Hack Jack taken off the album also did well in the independent charts. The album featured many classic tracks including an X rated version of Gene Vincent's classic Be Bop a Lula, the excellent Transvestite Blues and a manic cover of the old Osmond's song Crazy Horses it was a very impressive debut album and the band have recently followed it up with their next album Kicked Out Of Hell also on ID records.

At the time of the interview the new album had yet to be released. I managed to ask the bands singer Mark Phillips and the bands drummer Ant Thomas some questions about Demented Are Go. The interview was conducted at the Klub Foot in Hammersmith (RIP) just before the band's last performance there, before it was knocked down and made into a post office or car park or whatever. The first question I asked them was what do they think of their new album Kicked Out of Hell? Ant answers: "We're not happy with the mix, apart from that it's alright". Mark then replies: "The first demo was better than the album". Ant: "This one is alright, but it's just he only had two and a half days to mix it, cos of a bloody low budget and he just didn't have time to mix it. The first album we did had like a heavy metal producer at first and he was excellent, it had a really heavy sound and then Pete Gage done on the top of that, so it sounded alright, but this new one was a bit of a hurry. It will be good when it's out, we want to get the thing mixed again before it comes out". The band also had a cover designed for the album by the band's artist Simon Cohen, but the record company didn't use it, they used their own cover which the band are very disappointed about, as Ant says: "It's just a blank cover wait 'til you see it". The new album sees the vinyl debut of the band's new line up, which Ant comments: "At the moment we've got a line up we're sort of happy with". The new line up comes due to Dick Thomas the band's original guitarist leaving the band and the band having a steady influx of bass players, I wondered why Dick left the band, Ant answers: "He left to get married and all the rest". Mark: "Sell prunes in France". Ant: "He was going to sell prunes in France with his girlfriend who he was meant to be going to marry, he came back after a week in France. He's just fixing fridges or something in London now. Good guitarist but bit of a prat really". So how did the bands two new members come to join the band? The new members being Lex Luther on guitar and Graeme Grant on bass, Ant explains: "Graeme bought a treb off us at Camden market and came back and said I'm a Jelly do you want a bass player, so we went yeah, and Lex we met him drunk up here (Klub Foot) saying how good he was on guitar, so we said yeah alright come down tomorrow and we'll have an audition". Had any of the band played in any previous bands before? Mark replies: "Yeah, Lex was in The Bog Rats". Ant: "And Graeme was in some Rockabilly band The Chequers years ago, he was in them for a bit". and yourselves? Mark: "He was in a band, and I was in a band". Ant: "Oh yeah. he, (Mark) was in Nervous Breakdown that Rockabilly band, he used to drum with them". So, when did you first get into the Demented sound? Ant: "We were into Punk and then we was into Rockabilly and then it all got fashionable and we thought fuck this and we just went sick in the head".

Graeme the bands new bassist then walks into the interview, he looks across sees my tape recorder walks straight over to it and then says to it: "Ever seen a grown man in the nude?" strange cat! He then says: "What do you want to know? I'm mental". Ant then says: "He's the one who came back saying he's a Jelly". Graeme: "That was the first time I saw you". What happened to the bands outrageous stage act? Graeme answers: "The makeup was too dear, seriously the makeup was too dear half the time, and half the time you can't be bothered and in the end, we can't put it on properly so we just look like something that Steptoe's just dragged in, and we had a weird reaction of all of that, half of the people were into it". Mark: "I don't know I was really into it but no one else was". Graeme: "I did when I used to do my Vietnam and I used to come on as a Vet with my face all blown up by a napalm bomb, but after a while you run out of ideas. Mind you I saw wicked jacket today, it's like an early seventeenth century type Captain Poopdecker with the hat, you know them funny shaped hats that the old sailors wore press gang sort of outfit". Where did the band get the Rubber Buccaneer, Pervy in The Park style image from? Ant points to Mark: "It's just his warped head" he says. So, what was the original inspiration behind the band? Mark answers: "Get lots of money for drugs". Has it happened? "No" he replies. "We just into it for a laugh" Mark concludes. Ant: "We thought we would play a few gigs in Cardiff and that would be it". Do you like being described as a Psychobilly band? Graeme answers: "We're beyond that, we're not twiddly, you know what I mean?". Mark: "It's just a name anyway". Ant: "It's just a silly label". So how would you describe Demented Are Go? "Punk Rock 'n' Roll". Mark replies. Ant: "Psychedelic Punk Rock 'n' Roll with a bit of Hillbilly thrown in".

Going back to the subject of the bands outrageous stage act I wondered, whatever happened to the rubber doll the band used to have on stage with them? "Dead" Ant answers. "Yeah, twice I think" Mark replies. "And we've had two now, they're both dead. one got set fire to. He, Mark set fire to one in Cardiff, he swung it around his head for ten minutes and that was it, it was gone. But they just get punctured straight away, you can't repair them". How did the bands version of Be Bop a Lula come about? Ant answers: "At a practise Dick just started playing it and we all jammed along to it and then we just made it part of the set. That was one of the first songs we got together". How did loyal Gene Vincent fans take it? Mark answers: "I don't know, we've had some stick for it sometimes like". Ant: "I remember we played it to some Teddy Boys, and this one's for all the Teds down there it's called Be Bop A Lula and they just sort of went yeah, they got up and they started dancing, and then the song came in and they just went leave it out. It was hilarious". How, do you find playing gigs around England? Ant answers: "It depends where you go, if you go somewhere you're not sure of up North they're really into it. In Stoke it was great up there. I think in London it has really died it's only like the Klub Foot, anywhere else you don't see many people going". Do you find it better playing aboard? Mark answers: "Everybody does you know, you're treated better". Ant: "You get better treatment, it's cos you go over there and you're British. It's like we get top hotels, top food laid on, all the beer you can drink. But over here Klub Foot like we get one crate of them little cans of Skol, no food and you're on twice the money out there 'n all".

Apart from the two studio albums Demented Are Go were featured on they were also on the Sick Sick Sick live album on ID records, which mainly featured Demented along with a few tracks from Skitzo and The Coffin Nails. Mark explains his views on the album: "I thought it was a bit out of order for the people who like Demented. We didn't even know about it being released until about three or four months later". Ant: "They released that because Dick had left, and they thought let's make a fast buck out of Demented, so, that's why they released it. It was rushed mixed". The video of the band playing at the Klub Foot was also released, yet again entitled Sick Sick Sick. It was recorded at the same gig that the album was recorded at. What did the band think of it? Ant: "Not much really". Mark: "It was alright". Ant: "One day we heard that there's this video and record coming out. We heard the album; I didn't like it at all". Another live album the band were featured on was Stomping at The Klub Foot Volume Two. Did the band find it helped being featured on that album? Ant answers: "Yeah, it started rolling a bit after that. We hated them two songs we were so drunk that night it was just ridiculous. All the songs we wanted to play were just totally wrong, so we had to use 'Transvestite Blues' and 'Pickled and Preserved'. But we were going to play 'One Sharp Knife' and a couple of others, but we just couldn't". Would band like to produce their own records? Ant answers: " He (Mark) was good at it when we did the demo, he got all the effects going and that. I wouldn't have a clue".

The band's first ever vinyl release were two tracks on the Nervous Records compilation Hell's Bent on Rockin. The two tracks being Rubber Rock and One Sharp Knife, both tracks proved an excellent taster for the In Sickness and In Health album. The band sometimes still play the two songs in their live set. Ant explains how Demented came to being included on the compilation: "We had a couple of gigs with the GuanaBatz up in London, and he (Roy Williams) just phoned up one day. They're two of my favourite songs quite honestly". Pretty soon after that compilation, and after many successful gigs ID records became interested in the band, as Ant explains: "Dick sorted it out, I think. They'd seen us doing some supports up here after that Nervous Records compilation we done and they gave us the Stomping at The Klub Foot thing, and they gave us a deal straight after that". Then the band's debut album In Sickness and In Health was released and stormed up the independent charts getting to number nine. Were the band surprised at the success of the album? Ant answers: "Success? it went to number nine, yeah quite chuffed with that but didn't really sell a lot on record". Were the band surprised at how popular they were becoming? Mark answers: "Yeah, we were a bit really". Ant: "But it was a lot of work. It was two years before anyone knew of us. We were just playing in Cardiff for two years; we got a wicked following together".

Although the band were in the independent charts the music press virtually ignored them, not even bothering to review their album constructively, just judging the band through the image on the sleeve. In fact, reviewing it purely as Psychobilly and not even attempting to critique the music respectfully. Pretty pointless even bothering to write about it, with a one-sided view of rockin' music. But the fans proved the journalists wrong by getting the album into the independent top ten. Ant explains his view about the music press: "They're just failed musicians, music journalists not calling you one like, but people who do dodgy reviews of people in these music papers they've just been in bands before that don't make it and think oh well, I'll be a journalist and slag every other band off". Would the band ever change in terms of success? Mark answers: "We're going to change in our own way, we're not going to listen to anybody who's going to say got to be like this and that". Ant: "We formed our own sound anyway we don't sound like any of the other bands it's like we formed this and we're just following that".

Did the band find it harder to get themselves established as they come from Wales? Ant answers: "It took a while to get into it". Mark: "Not really 'cos we're up here (in London)". Ant: "We all live in London 'cos in the end we were playing in London more than we was playing in Cardiff, so we just thought we might as well move up". In their live set the band sometimes use a violinist as Ant explains: "He's on the new album, he's the geezer who used to play for Sunglasses After Dark - Simon Cohen, he's a good geezer, he's done all our T shirts". Simon Cohen also designed the sleeves for the Blood on The Cats series of compilation albums on Anagram Records, he also designed the cover which the band wanted to use on their Kicked Out of Hell album. I then asked Mark and Ant what their favourite Demented Are Go songs are, Ant: "One Sharp Knife and Holy Hack Jack are mine". Mark: "Pervy in the Park". Ant: "And Sick Spasmiod which will be on the new l.p.". Song writing for the band as Ant explains: "Is done by Mark and Graeme writes a few as well. Mark writes the lyrics". Mark: "Most of them not all of them". For the future the band have planned to: "Just keep it going" as Ant explains. Mark: "Surf to oblivion". So, before the interview is finished is there anything else that the band would like to say? Ant: "Buy the album".

Whilst the interview was being conducted at the bar of the Klub Foot before the loud p.a. system interrupted us, Simon Brand from Torment came over to say hello to Demented and join in the chat. I never included his comments in the original article due to it being totally focused on Demented. So, for the first time here is Simon Brand initially discussing his then recent tour of Germany: "Germany, it was a laugh much better than the gigs last year, but I would have liked to see more people, but the people who did come it was really, really appreciated, we went to Berlin, it was amazing". Simon then explains the pressures of being in a band: "We just got a problem being in a band really, its real pressure, it's easier going to work, less hassle. We haven't practised since last time we played here. We've only done two songs and we were supposed to book up a studio to start next weekend when we are all free. We're supposed to record an album. This album we're doing is supposed to be a mini album and a 12" single this year". The recordings Simon was talking about later became the bands third album 'Round the World' released on Nervous Records in 1989. Simon mentions Roy Williams of Nervous Records: "Good as gold Roy, lets us do what we want. We've got a studio in Bristol, our own producer and that's it, just send him the tape afterwards and he pays all the money".

Simon then talks about Frenzy who he had previously been a member of: "I had a practise with Frenzy last week. Steve (Whitehouse) wanted me to join Frenzy. I went over for a practise with Adam (Seviour)". Simon stated that Frenzy: "Play everything so perfect, you have to concentrate, so I said I'm not interested. He's a good bass player, he's into Bros as well!". Ant enquires what happened to Frenzy's guitarist Kevin Saunders, Simon answers: "Teaching guitar, he's packed it all in".

Simon then gave his view concerning the UK Psychobilly scene at the time, is its popularity fading? "I think it is you know in England; we just don't get any gigs". Ant: "Sometimes you get gigs and there's loads of people and the rest of the time you go to gigs and there is like fifty people there who just stand there and watch you. That Rayleigh gig there was about ten people in it, the geezer who ran the place gave us four hundred quid to play it. I felt sorry for the geezer, at the end he said you going to do me a favour then? and we went no". Simon: "We played Shelley's in Lowestoft you go on this little pier it was miles away, we went there January/February, waves all over the place, freezing cold, pissing down with rain. There was about fifteen people there and it was a massive place, bigger than the Klub Foot, he paid us two hundred and fifty quid". Ant: "It's better abroad". Simon: "In Germany, I was surprised it's going downhill". Ant: "We were there filling the places". Simon: "We was there in May; it was just a vibe it just seems like England a year ago. It seems like people are losing interest a bit. I mean there are no new bands". Simon then asks me if I am in a band. "I mean whether you like them or not Restless are good and they're different and Frenzy and you (Demented) but bands that get on now, they are like kids from the audience, who can play three chords on the guitar". Simon then discusses his musical journey: "I just want to get into blues. It's easier to play Chuck Berry covers or that, it's ace".

Then the p.a. blasted out and the interview resumed with Mark and Ant in the Klub Foot toilets. Demented Are Go emerged into becoming one of the leading Psychobilly bands throughout the world whose popularity has remained even to this day. The quality of their albums has remained consistently strong throughout the years, and they are still a very popular live act. Mark (now known as Sparky) featured on a duet with the Swiss band The Hillbilly Moon Explosion entitled 'My Love for Evermore' which at the time of writing has had over 21,000,000 YouTube views. Nick Kemp also wrote a fantastic biography of the band 'Kicked Out of Hell'. To state that the band have gained legendary status within the Psychobilly scene would not be an understatement. Sadly, Simon Brand is no longer with us.

Bios from bands.

I started to receive bios from bands, featuring a few photos for hopeful inclusion in The Crazed. If the fanzine had continued these would have been useful to use as background for future interviews. I decided to include a couple of these bios in issue four. Two bands had sent me material that I thought would make interesting and informative additions to the issue. The Radium Cats and The Lost Souls. Both bands were starting to establish themselves on the scene, but with the imminent closure of the Klub Foot it was obviously going to be more difficult for them than the bands who had regularly played there and had gained a following by doing so. Both these bands had great potential and released albums on Nervous that were popular within the diminishing scene

The Lost Souls.

The Lost Souls were first formed in 1985, when a group of old friends got together just for laughs. It was a four-piece band then with the drummer Mick, slap bass player Broomie, guitarist Nick and vocalist Paul. As '85 came and went so did the gigs and it was soon obvious that the line-up wasn't working, so at the beginning of '86 The Lost Souls saw their first change in line-up with new guitarist Pete joining the band. This was the start to a good gigging year when they played with top bands such as Frenzy, GuanaBatz and King Kurt.

After making a demo at a local studio they were offered to put two songs on a compilation album with Raucous Records and also managed to get interest from Roy Williams of Nervous Records after sending him a tape. Just as the band started to get somewhere Pete the newest member left, taking the vocalist with him.

Despite the setbacks the slap bass player Broomie who had originally formed The Lost Souls sought after a new guitarist in March '88, one was found Neil, with this a new direction for the band was sought. So, at this time the old drummer was replaced with the new talent of Steve.

With the new changes in the band came a new sound, from the almost Rockabilly Jump sound came a new exciting raunchy Psychobilly noise.

The influences differ from member to member. Steve the drummer is into Pete Barnacle from Spear of Destiny and Rat Scabies from The Damned. The guitarist Neil on the other hand prefers a much more fifties sound with original Rock 'n' Roll crossed with the fast guitar of P Paul Fenech from The Meteors. The bass player Broomie prefers the proper Psychobilly sound of Frenzy with Steve Whitehouse, Sam from the Batz and the original Delta's sound.

All the band prefer the original Psychobilly scene of '85/'86 and so they would say their place will be up in the running with the best Frenzy, The Meteors and the Batz, which The Lost Souls feel Psychobilly was all about, whereas now it's a much more Psycho Punk sound.

The major ambitions for The Lost Souls are to get lots of gigs, loads of money and to be a household name in Psychobilly.

The Radium Cats.

Edinburgh based The Radium Cats describe their style of music as Voodoo Punkabilly which to anyone who has seen the band or heard the band's album would agree is a fair description of their manic yet controlled style of Psychobilly. The band are a three-piece and as I wrote previously come for Edinburgh where they've gained a loyal and ever growing following. The band consists of brothers Paul Paterson (guitar, vocals) and Lee Paterson (double bass, vocals) along with Johnny Maben a Psycho Punkabilly drummer of the same mould as the other band members, as their biography says.

The band were formed in the summer of '86 by Paul and Lee along with what they describe as a drummer from the rockin' scene. Although the two brothers had played in several rockin' bands before. The actual first Radium Cats line up saw its first appearance in the Summer of '86. The band decided to go on the road around Scotland and went down well with their frantic performances. They supported such bands as the Styng Rites and Blues 'n' Trouble. They gained such a good reputation that since November '86 the band have headlined at virtually all their gigs and have also claimed to be the only one real Psychobilly band left in Scotland. Soon after Christmas '86 the band introduced a new drummer into their line up a more manic sounding drummer, this being Dean Robertson. The new line up played their first gig at Edinburgh University's Potterow on 30th of January, the new line up was a success, the band played to an enormous crowd and two weeks later were invited to play at the University's Wilkie house on 13th of February alongside We Free Kings and the Dog Faced Hermans. The gig pulled in four hundred people and showed that there would be no stopping the band, as over the next few months they gigged extensively included playing in front of one thousand people at the Moud, Edinburgh and also a gig which will probably be looked back upon as a classic at the Edinburgh venue, due to the band bringing over a litre of theatrical blood on stage which although the audience loved it the people who run the club didn't and banned the band from playing there.

Along the way the band attracted Fast Forward to approach the band about recording a single, but due to various reasons the band had to part company with drummer Dean and therefore due to no drummer didn't get to record their debut single. Trying to find a new drummer to fill the space Dean left in the band proved an arduous task, as all the drummers the band auditioned seemed unsuitable. Getting frustrated with the line-up situation Lee and Paul took to busking around the streets, which mainly featured the band performing a few Rockabilly covers. They were offered to play Festival Fringe but declined as they explained that Rockabilly covers wasn't what The Radium Cats were about. After a lot of auditioning the band eventually found a suitable drummer Johnny Mabon, enter the present line up.

The new line up started gigging in November and December of '87 which included a return gig at The Venue with The Pharaohs, this time with no theatrical blood, as the band decided to no longer use it. The band also entered the recording studio during early '88 to start work on their debut album Munster Madness for Mental Records, which is now out and includes eight tracks ranging from covers of old classics like Long Black Train, Go Go Go to the bands own compositions like (I Hear it) Howling in the Swamp, Jungle Drums and you've just got to hear the bands excellent Screaming from the Grave. "Our debut album Munster Madness is selling extremely well, in fact the first pressing sold out within the first few weeks" explains Lee. "The release of the mini album fulfils the bands obligation to Mental Records, and we are at present considering offers from English record companies. With this the band recently demoed a number of original songs including Six Foot Down, Strange Baby Strange and Plan 9 from Outer Space". Lee continues: "Being based almost four hundred miles North The Radium Cats are not influenced by the London Psychobilly scene, and we feel that we have developed a sound and style of our own. The bands musical influences come from the weird fifties' artists such as Herbie Duncan, Charlie Feathers, Screamin' Jay Hawkins and Gene Ross (the bands live set currently includes a cover of Endless Sleep. Lyrically the band look to fifties sci fi movies and American 'twist in the tale' comic books such as Astounding Stories and Weird Tales". If you hope to catch the band at a gig, Lee says: "We are currently lining up some dates in England". So, it seems that The

Radium Cats are a band to look out for in the future. So, look out for future record releases by the band and gigs as they've now established themselves around Scotland and believe it's time for the rest of England. That is at least if they're not all Howling in the Swamp. Aaaaarrrrgggghhhhh!

The Caravans.

I managed to arrange an interview with The Caravans who had just released their Easy Money album on Nervous Records which I liked and featured some great songs which displayed the bands strong song writing skills. I thought The Crazed would benefit from an interview with the band, who fortunately agreed to be interviewed before their appearance at Dingwalls in Camden Town.

Having been featured previously in issue two of The Crazed, The Caravans have certainly been busy since my last article. Bob Taylor the band's lead guitarist at the time left the band to be replaced by Rich Caso who previously played in Get Smart. The band eventually released their debut album on Nervous Records entitled Easy Money. The album showed a more mature polished sound than their previous releases on various compilation albums. The following interview was conducted just before the band were due to perform at lunch time at Dingwalls in Camden Town. The interview took place with the band and myself plus Marcus Heywood The Crazed roadie sitting outside Dingwalls looking upon Camden Lock, all very scenic I'm sure you would agree. Anyway, first question seems quite obvious what do the band think about their album Easy Money? Mark Penington the bands singer and double bass player answers: "We're quite pleased with it. We're pleased with the production, but the playing could have been a lot better, it's not as tight as we'd have liked it, but that's what happened on the day". So how long did it take to record? Mark: "It took us about six weeks altogether, but it was only done at weekends, sort of like every weekend and one bank holiday weekend". I noticed that the album was produced by the band themselves as Mark explains: "When we actually do the final mix down, I was the one there to do the album and I had like 99% over what went on. The only thing I didn't do was twiddle the knobs that was Chris Sutton who engineered it he's a brilliant engineer, he's one of the best. I mean if he makes us sound good, he's got to be good". The sound quality of the album certainly complemented The Caravans sound. Would Mark like to get more involved in the production side of records? "Well, it's early days yet". Mark answers: "I really haven't got enough experience in being in a recording studio to actually go in and actually do it all, but I'd love to do that". Need it be strictly rockin' music? "I'll stick with the sort of music I like, I mean if I like some other sort of music and some band approached me about it, I'd obviously like to do it but unless I like the music in the first, I wouldn't have anything to do with it".

Apart from producing the album Mark also wrote a majority of the songs on the album, does he regard himself as the main songwriter of the band? "Yeah, the main songwriter, yeah. I don't write all of them there's one or two tracks on the album that we all wrote, the initial idea came from someone else, and we all put it in. A lot of the stuff we do is like an idea, and everyone sort of like chips in. We all have different ideas how the songs sound and the end result is a whole lot different than what it starts off as, as that's just the way it happens". Where do you get the influences from for your song writing? Mark: "Influences and song writing? anything and everything it's not any one thing it's everything and anything. it might be a song from Top of The Pops I might think that that sounds good".

Bob Taylor the bands original lead guitarist used to write some of the band's early songs along with Mark. How did it affect the band when he left? Mark explains: "He was a great guitarist, and he was good for us at the time. He decided he wanted to go to college instead. It affected the band in a way because we got better, because everything clicked a lot easier, everything seemed to happen more freely than trying to force it. We did a lot of song writing together, but mainly the ideas came from either one or the two of us, and the stuff that we're doing now is a lot different to the stuff me and Bob were writing together in the first place. A lot of the stuff that me and Bob wrote together didn't work and wouldn't work live because his ideas were a lot different to mine. The songs we played live and recorded which were mainly written by me, Brian and the rest of them". A boat then passes through Camden lock with a load of tourists on board, for some reason or the other they all start clapping, Brian Gilman the bands rhythm guitarist jokes: "Damn good interview that". Anyhow, back to the interview. Rich Caso replaced Bob on lead guitar. I asked Rich what he thinks he's introduced into the band's sound: "Me, myself, personally?" he asks. "I don't really know. The band is to my preference, because we've all got different ideas and we're all not run of the mill Rockabilly. At the moment it's getting me a bit down because well I don't know why we're not falling into a category. People have watched us and they don't know what to think of us. When we play down the Klub Foot we always go down well there. The band is good because we're like a band, I mean me and Lee like a lot of varied stuff and we don't really look the part and act the part it's good".

The Caravans have been described as sounding like an authentic Rockabilly band. The band explain their views on this: "It's our authentic" answers Brian. Mark: "I mean there's different tones in authentic Rockabilly, it's the way you play it, it's not the final sound. In the fifties if they could have got a compact disc sound, I'm sure they would have done. It's the way you played; it wouldn't have all been bodged. I mean they wouldn't have deliberately bodged it to make it sound right. I mean if they had the equipment and the engineers to do it in those days it would have sounded like some of the bands today, sort of like Red Hot 'n' Blue sound it sounds authentic, but it also sounds very well done. I mean their one and only album is great". But what about The Caravans being described in a certain category? Mark: "I'm doing my politician bit now; I'm answering questions without.... no, we obviously are a modern Rockabilly band, I mean we're not all sort of like forty-five years old. I love authentic Rockabilly that's what I'm into, but it's how it comes out, it's how you play it, it's not the way it's produced or the way it sounds on the night, it's how you play it. I wouldn't like to be described as anything, we're just a band playing what we play and if people like to describe us as an authentic Rockabilly band, then it's up to them, if they want to describe us as modern Rockabilly that's also up to them". But don't you think the inclusion of a double bass into a bands line up makes some people automatically wrongly dismiss a band as a fifties revival band? Mark: "Not necessarily, I hate bass guitars and I couldn't even think about playing bass guitars. I mean the double bass obviously gives it an acoustic sound; I wouldn't say it's authentic to any extent. I mean there's bands using acoustic instruments now that sound modern but are using acoustic instruments that are sort of like twenty-five to thirty years old, but they still sound modern because of the way it's being produced".

Do the band find it a restriction playing rockin' music, like finding gigs around the country? Mark answers: "It's not harder to find gigs, the thing is if you're a Rockabilly band you're playing the music because you want to, you don't play it because you're deliberately trying to get somewhere, you're playing it because you want to and the people who want to listen go to the gigs where you play. You don't sort of say oh yeah, I want to play at Hammersmith Odeon because if you want to play at Hammersmith Odeon, if the people that like that sort of music go to Hammersmith Odeon, we'll probably end up playing there one day. But you play where people want to listen to you". Would the band ever consider changing their sound if it meant more exposure and attracting an audience that would fill Hammersmith Odeon? Mark answers: "Depends how big the change was, the music we play is just what we play, we don't deliberately try to play anything". So, you might consider it? Mark: "Dunno, not unless we enjoy playing it. We're not going to play what we don't want to play; we play what we like".

Lee Barnett the bands drummer then appears, now, here is someone who has appeared on Blind Date. I couldn't really finish the interview without asking him about it, although I'm probably not the first person to ask, as he answers: "Oh no, why do you want to know about that then? ask me a specific question then. I went on Blind Date for a laugh, I think that's all. I only did it for a laugh. I didn't write off or anything like that it was my manager put me in for it". Rich: "He got more fame out of that than he ever did with The Caravans and he didn't even mention us". Mark: "He called us a local band". Lee: "Cos they said no advertising and stuff like that. They would have just rubbed it out if I had said anything like that". Then the interview finishes, and the band go into Dingwalls and perform their set featuring songs from their Easy Money album. Definitely a band to watch out for on the rockin' scene.

The Caravans went on to release many albums. The band managed to appeal to both Rockabilly and Psychobilly crowds and always maintained their style throughout some line-up changes and even dabbled in Psychobilly on the No Mercy album which featured a song called Psychobilly Pop Star.

The Quakes.

The first time I heard The Quakes music was in Hummingbird Records a long-gone record shop in Ramsgate, as soon as I entered the shop and started flicking through the Rock 'n' Roll/Rockabilly section Pack Our Bags and Go (a track from the band's debut album) started blasting through the shop's speakers. I was impressed and quickly purchased the album. The band had arrived in London from Buffalo, New York and had brought their own unique, frantic and aggressive Psychobilly with them. I soon arranged an interview with the band outside Dingwalls, Camden Town. The band were friendly and approachable with singer and guitarist Paul Roman emerging as the spokesman for the band. They came across as enthusiastic, eager and hungry for respect and recognition within the scene. After the interview they kindly posed by Camden Lock for a photo session. Just before I was due to transcribe the interview and feature it in issue four of The Crazed the band had split with bass player Rob-O-Peltier and drummer Dave 'The Ace' Hoy returning to America whilst Paul Roman stayed in London. I remember speaking to Paul at the Klub Foot, he cut a solitary figure without the rest of the group, but he did agree to write the reasons for the bands split for issue four which replaced the interview. Sadly Dave 'The Ace' Hoy died later in a car accident.

The Quakes lived a very short but explosive life on the Psychobilly scene, bringing their double bass, Gretsch guitar and drum kit all the way from their native Buffalo, New York. They played their own crazy manic style of Psychobilly American style. They impressed audiences abroad at Psychobilly festivals and especially proving a great hit with German Psychobilly's, in fact Roy Williams (head of Nervous Records) wrote after he saw the band perform at the second Belgium Psychobilly festival "These guys were great! A sort of Psychobilly Stray Cats, surely, they must make a record soon!". Which they ended up doing for Roy's very own Nervous Records, the album simply being called The Quakes, Whilst the band were recording their debut, they performed at the Klub Foot which proved a successful if somewhat chaotic gig. The album was finally released by Nervous with Doc Stewart at the controls and featured a cover very reminiscent of the first Stray Cats album cover. The tracks on the album showed that all the anticipation for the band had been justified as it was a great debut with some classic tracks such as Hangman's Noose, The Deal and Where Did it Go? to mention a few. The album was received well. The band played some more gigs and had lined up another European tour but then split within a few months after they had established their name.

Lead singer and guitarist of the band Paul Roman explains why The Quakes split, the other two members he refers to being Rob-O-Peltier on double bass and Dave 'The Ace' Hoy on drums. "We were in London living in a one-bedroom flat in Bow, there was nothing to do and we had no money, we lived on £2.50 a day to feed all three of us. Because we were in each other's contact twenty-four hours a day, we got on each others nerves, but they didn't take it like a professional they took it personally. I told them that even if we hated each other we could go up on stage and rock. I also told them early on that I was going to make it whether they were with me or not. Finally, it came down to a big argument in the West End, our European tour was cancelled because the German promotor fucked it all up. We were in debt and things were tense, I told the both of them that things like this happen to bands all the time and it's something you have to live with and move on. They complained and complained and put some of the blame on me for the tour. I told them plain and simple if you don't like it here then go home, then a few days later they came in and started packing and they just left, just like that".

"We were going places fast and we were booked for a festival in Sheffield over bands such as The Frantic Flintstones and others that have been here a long time and done loads of gigs. Also upcoming in March, the fourth Psycho Festival in Belgium, we were booked second only to King Kurt who are reforming for the gig. We were better live than most groups and we would have challenged Restless, The Meteors and the Batz with time. They (the band) threw it all away, any way I refuse to give up. My new band is called Paul Roman and The Prowlers, featuring Nick Peck on bass ex Rattlers and Gavin Smith on drums ex Nitros, the emphasis is on Rock'n' Roll, wild

Rock 'n' Roll. Yes, we are doing some Quakes stuff and the odd Rattlers number. I have also recorded two songs for Nervous Records by myself (overdubbing). I play bass. I taught Rob bass and I taught Dave drums, my music will always be wild not Pop. I had to change the style there's no way I could get replacements for Rob and Dave and still have it sound the same. People don't realise we'd been together two years....well okay, one and a half years before we came here and you can't fill that spot with someone you hardly know. I also feel a need to return to my Rockabilly roots, don't get me wrong we weren't doing Psycho to make Dollars I felt that music and I love it. I not only go to the Klub Foot but also to rockin' clubs. To me it's all rockin' but in this country it's so separate, I want to bridge the gap with this band".

So, there you have it the official story behind The Quakes split. Watch out for Pauls new band Paul Roman and The Prowlers who will be touring pretty soon.

Paul later reformed The Quakes with Rob-O-Peltier and released the excellent Voice of America album on Nervous Records which displayed a maturity and advancement of their sound and song writing. The band are still gigging and releasing exciting records today. Paul Roman later explained to me: "We have not been a huge success but that has also allowed me to do whatever I want without fear of losing fans. My music is all over the "abilly" spectrum and I like to try new things". Long may he continue with whatever incarnation of The Quakes he has formed.

The Krewmen top ten.

The Krewmen provided their favourite top ten records, although the choices provided were for the band and not the individual members.

TallBoys: Another Half Hour till Sunrise.

Elvis Presley: Money Honey.

Stray Cats: Rock This Town.

King Kurt: Billy.

Billy Idol: White Wedding.

Buddy Holly: Peggy Sue.

Motorhead: Ace of Spades.

The Polecats: Rockabilly Guy.

Matchbox: Rockabilly Rebel.

Gary Glitter: Leader of the Gang.

Letter from Oggie.

Skitzo's manager Oggie also provided me with an update about the band which I included in the issue:

Hi,

I thought I better write a bit on Skitzo. We recorded Terminal Damage at Touchsound Studios. We met Peter the engineer and explained to him the sound we wanted, he was great he understood and made everybody relaxed, which I believe is a start on making everybody bring out their musical talent. Obviously, the sound is a bit different to Skitzo Mania, but I believe we have the ultimate sound. It took about six days to do the recording, unfortunately we were on holiday for the final mix but Peter the engineer went along just to keep an eye on things, the end result – brilliant.

Just had some letters offering gigs in Spain, France, Germany, Belgium, Switzerland and Austria, hope I can work these out. One way of getting old and grey with bad nerves = be a manager of Skitzo!

The end of The Crazed.

Issue four was completed, it included no introduction as there was really nothing to say. I knew it was the final issue and it looked more like a pamphlet than a fanzine whereas issues two and three had covers that were printed on coloured paper, issue four did not it was just plain white. I had also included the words 'final issue' on the cover. I don't remember how many copies I had printed but it was the smallest print run of all the issues. I was still happy with the content of it, but no longer wanted to produce it as the initial enthusiasm I had when I started the fanzine had dissipated just like the Psychobilly scene that I had so loved. Looking back, it was a mistake as quite a few of the bands continued and some great records were to be released. The scene where I lived had virtually gone, people had moved or were no longer into it. The closure of the Klub Foot had a massive impact and when it moved to The Boston Arms it felt a mere shadow of its former self, I remember seeing The Radium Cats on stage and although they were a great band it felt like the magic of the Klub Foot had gone forever. Just before the Klub Foot closed I remember selling the fanzine outside the venue and approaching a Psychobilly couple whom I asked if they would like to buy a copy for 50p, after all these years I remember the lad looking at me and scoffing that it cost 50p, I remember thinking this is your scene, the bands in this fanzine are your bands why would you not want to read about them, his attitude left a nasty impression on me. Also I attempted to interview Sam and Diddle from the GuanaBatz on one of the final nights at the Klub Foot only to be joined by another interviewer from a fanzine he was hoping to release . The other interviewer seemed to find it a competition and attempted to show off, I just couldn't be bothered with that, we are all into the scene and we should all stick together, and Sam and Diddle were great blokes why would I want to show off in front of them. Things did look like they might improve when the Town and Country Club in Kentish Town held a Psychobilly night with the GuanaBatz headlining. I remember walking up Camden High Street before the legendary gig with an old mate Phil donning a red baseball jacket, when I noticed a figure in front of me furtively crouching behind some parked cars, suddenly this person leapt out from behind the cars and grabbed me and wouldn't let me move, I remember Phil was completely oblivious and continued to walk up the high street with his glaring red baseball jacket getting further and further away. I was incapacitated and struggling to break free until I recognised the culprit to be Jonny Bowler formerly of Get Smart and now drummer for the GuanaBatz who was laughing at my temporary distress. That gig for me seemed to be the last really great Psychobilly gig at the time and unfortunately seemed to bring an unexpected closure of the great memories we all had of the Klub Foot, whose closing had a huge effect on me, I loved that venue and nothing for me at the time could live up to it. All scenes burn out, but Psychobilly kept the embers burning never quite getting extinguished. It spread its Psychotic roots throughout the world, even infecting the original birthplace of Rockabilly - the USA, but without The Crazed chronicling it.

The Crazed interviews again!

Here are some additional interviews I've conducted whilst writing and compiling this book, in a way you could say they make up an issue five. I hope you enjoy them.

Woodie Taylor.

Woodie Taylor was an early Meteors follower who ended up drumming for the band after original drummer Mark Robertson left. He was featured playing drums on the classic Meteors single 'Mutant Rock' which also featured the brilliant 'Hills Have Eyes' as the b side. After The Meteors Woodie joined former Meteors band mates Nigel Lewis and Mark Robertson in The Escalators and recorded the legendary album 'Moving Staircases'. He was also in the original line up of The Tall Boys. Woodie's story during this period is an essential piece of Psychobilly history. He agreed to do a telephone interview with me.

Woodie started his musical career by playing drums for Croydon Punk band The Daleks: "I was a Punk into The Clash, The Jam, The Damned and The Ruts". This changed when the lead singer of The Daleks went to see The Rezillos up at the Marquee and met a girl who was a hairdresser and lived in Harrow. "There was a lot of Rockabilly's from Harrow for whatever reason, and she used to cut quiffs and Mac Curtis haircuts". The Daleks singer trusted her to "cut his hair in a quiff". It was 1979 and the Spirit of Punk was fading, and Woodie was looking for a new image: "I think there were a lot of Punks by that time who were just a bit bored with spiky hair and that second wave of Punk was coming through, I couldn't identify with that and generally I've always been into a progression of music rather than keeping it the same". The Daleks singer was now an item with the hairdresser so Woodie: "Asked his girlfriend if she would cut my hair the same. My hair was shorter and straighter than his and she said it wouldn't work, you should have a Mac Curtis and I was like what's that? she explained and gave me a flat top".

By the Summer of 1980 Woodie: "Had the haircut but I didn't have any music to identify with. I knew it was a Rockabilly haircut and I did have one of those Pickwick Records compilations called 'Rockabilly Dynamite' and Gene Vincent I got a little bit into that".

It wasn't until August 1980 that Woodie found what he had been looking for: "The Stray Cats headed to London, I saw them and that was it, they were my band. There were a couple of months where they were playing these small venues, I saw them a couple of times. They were just amazing no one could touch them really, they did it perfectly. They were a kind of Punky Rockabilly it just sat perfectly with what I wanted". But alas it wouldn't last as Woodie explains that by: "March 1981, they were massive everywhere. They went to Japan on a World tour, and they just disappeared". This created a: "Void of having a band I could go to see and that was the point The Meteors came along into my life".

The Meteors being home grown were creating their own mutated rockin' sound. These were the legendary days that arguably created the birth of Psychobilly and Woodie was there. "I guess I first heard of The Meteors from some guys from where I lived in Croydon. I can't remember the specific conversation, but I remember being aware of the band. I was going to see them at the Hope and Anchor but the person I was meeting didn't turn up. I eventually got to see them at The Marquee one Sunday evening with my girlfriend at the time and they were just amazing. They were really worried they were going to run on too long as there were strict rules about being on for your allotted amount of time otherwise you would be penalised. They just went through their set, it took about half an hour, and they did about ten encores, it was just incredible they just kept coming back and the encores were like the Rollin' Rock singles. There was a label they did some demos for; I think it was EMI it's like the earliest recordings and there were lots and lots of cover versions and that's the kind of stuff they played and that's how I came by The Meteors".

Woodie got more into The Meteors and rockin': "The thing I love about Rockabilly and certainly the less conventional Rockabilly records is where they are playing about with the echo. The guitar on Johnny Burnette Trio's Train Kept a Rollin' is quite avant garde it's not exactly strumming or even picking, with the Octaves it's quite unique. I remember being into that Johnny Burnette album the Rock 'n' Roll Trio one, great songs and brilliant production it was the raw and quirkier side of Rockabilly that I latched onto. I didn't like the straightlaced stuff. Obviously, that was going to take me down the route of what The Meteors were singing about, the sci fi and b movie stuff. It wasn't political, there was a cartoon element to it but also there was that thing to latch onto, I guess what ultimately became the Zorch thing". Woodie started feeling he was entering into a new culture: "We could feel we were from somewhere else. I remember when The Meteors supported 999 at The Lyceum maybe May 1981 and there must have been three dozen or less Rockabilly's or Psychobilly's as we were, and it felt quite elitist".

Woodie discusses The Meteors seminal debut album In Heaven: "Brilliant songs really, it was pretty well captured on that album. The track The Crazed from the moment I heard them play it, I think it was in Birmingham, those opening chords they still give me goose bumps, it's a brilliant song it really is I think it still stands up now, it's powerful. I remember Nigel saying he didn't have the actual album, but he had a test pressing of side two and his favourite Meteors song was Death Dance which I thought was quite interesting because it's one of Paul's, but it wasn't typical of Paul's songs the faster more Rockabilly ones he'd do so well". Woodie further explains Paul's contribution within the band, as he has a unique insight as he joined the band after original drummer Mark Robertson left: "It was almost effortless, I don't know when he wrote those songs, it was just something he could do, it was almost effortless the way he did it". The band released a three-track single under the pseudonym of The Clapham South Escalators, as Woodie explains: "That came out under a different guise, I mean Paul's song Leave Me Alone is a great Psychedelic pop song, how natural that sounded for Paul to do something like that, the harmonies the Psychedelia type of guitar, I mean what an amazing guitarist and he could turn his hand to it. I don't think I ever saw him practice ever and I used to hang out with him quite a lot". Woodie discusses the dynamic behind the legendary line-up: "I feel the original idea was Nigel's that he wanted to make a band like a UK version of The Cramps but more Rockabilly than Punk. I think Nigel found Paul a bit hard going but he was such a good guitarist, they had a great respect for one another. There was also a lot of laughter, a lot of joking. Nigel was a very quiet guy; he wasn't so involved in all that it was more Paul and the guys who followed him. Paul was just one of the guys".

As stated, Woodie joined The Meteors: "Right at the end of 1981. I had been able to join my favourite group and to be with them at a point that was very exciting because Mark Robertson had done all the hard work and I walked in and we were playing much bigger gigs and it was really exciting. The first gig I played was at the beginning of January, so we did January, February, March, April we played lots of gigs. We probably played thirty gigs in that period or at least twenty. There was a lot going on. We did the recordings Mutant Rock and Hills Have Eyes and also what became the second part of the Teenagers from Outer Space album". That compilation album also included 'Island of Lost Souls' a single which featured Nigel and Woodie and released under the name The Tall Boys. "The Island of Lost Souls is another example of a song Nigel had written that did kind of fit in with The Meteors. We didn't perform it live I don't think, but it worked well in the studio. It would have gone on an album and that other recording Another Half Hour till Sunrise (the b side which included Paul on guitar) to me is like a definitive Meteors recording". Another song on the Teenagers from Outer Space album: "Dog Eat Robot which we started playing as The Meteors and I don't think Paul kind of liked that kind of thing. I think Nigel would have liked to have been a lot more experimental at that point".

The Meteors original manager Nick Garrard played an integral part in the early days of the band: "Paul and Nick Garrard never really got on, they kind of tolerated each other at best, but they all kind of needed each other. Nick was fantastic with the graphic side of things, all the flyers and promotion. He was the guy to make all the contacts to make Meteor Madness (a short film of the band featuring a young Keith Allen). He does not get enough credit for his role; he was a quarter of the band at the time. Paul didn't want him around and by getting me his friend in the band it shifted the balance of power towards him. I was eighteen or nineteen and quite impressionable. We were in agreement that maybe Nick had taken the band as far as he could, this was about April 1982 and we went to see John Curd who was interested in managing the band. We all agreed to Nick being sacked but neither Nigel or Paul wanted to do it, so I did it, it was on the first anniversary of me seeing The Meteors for the first time, from not even knowing who they were to sacking the manager". The dynamic quickly changed within the band: "Paul assumed control. There was only one gig that Nigel played after Nick had been sacked and he just thought I've had enough of this and that's basically what happened".

Nigel's departure had left a big impact on the band: "From one week we are selling out The Marquee to the following week where we are playing the 100 Club to about fifty people. John Curd the promotor who started the Klub Foot and WXYZ Records got The Meteors support on the Anti Nowhere League UK tour I think August 1982. He could see that Punks would like The Meteors and Paul would appeal to these people and that's exactly what happened, that's where the audience came from. After that Anti Nowhere League thing John Curd put on a Halloween gig at The Lyceum and The Meteors headlined. It took about six months to build it all up again and that was probably the reason why I stayed in the band after Nigel left because I was friends with Paul, although I felt that The Meteors to me were Paul and Nigel together". Woodie now felt it was time to leave his once favourite band: "When Nigel left The Meteors in a way that was it for me because I thought the magic of The Meteors was Paul and Nigel together and they really complimented one another. It just wasn't the same after Nigel had gone. I was Paul's mate and I stuck by him, but I wasn't prepared to give up my day job and I had my girlfriend in Clapham at the time to go on tour with the Anti Nowhere League, it wasn't the direction I wanted to go in". Woodie now back to being a fan of Psychobilly gravitated towards: "King Kurt in 1982 in the post Meteors void I fell into. I think King Kurt helped me through that period, it was a little bit more fun. They put on cheap nights in Clapham where I lived".

It wasn't long before Woodie fell back into Nigel Lewis' orbit: "At the time I was quite into the idea of getting better as a guitarist and I had played with this band who had supported The Meteors a few times called Fear, a kind of Punky band that were formed by a few people who were quite early Meteors followers and Mark Robertson played drums originally as he was friendly with these guys. We played the 100 Club in October 1981 before I joined The Meteors and Adam Skeaping who had recorded Radioactive Kid did a live recording of that show. Nigel went into hospital for a back operation and he had that live cassette and said that he had liked the guitar I had done on that and I remember going to see him in hospital and offering my services. I had seen his new band The Escalators a couple of times and that's how I got in. The Escalators all happened quite quickly. My involvement wasn't probably much more than a year". The band released a classic album called Moving Staircases on Big Beat Records and a couple of singles including one which featured The Munsters theme tune as the b side: "Moving Staircases to be honest a few people have come up to me and said that's their favourite ever album. At the time I was mourning the loss of The Meteors and to me The Escalators was just something I was doing. There were two guys in the band who play guitar better than I could, it was a bit daunting to be honest. There is probably only one song on that album where I think there was a little spark in my guitar playing which might have been the kind of thing Nigel had been interested in and that's Dog Eat Robot, I do a little kind of lead riff. I think the songs I like best on that album are songs I play drums with Mark Robertson on, stuff like Flanders Fields, Survivalists, Cut Up and The Day the Sun Burnt Down, Mark and I played stuff to complement each other. I think the album flows well it needs all the different tracks to make sense. The Munsters theme was a b side, and it was made into a double a side, it started bubbling under the top 100, it was a big thing on that alternative disco scene. It appealed to variety of different kids. For me The Escalators was very much an in between band for me and there was a thing about my hair I was going through an anti-Psychobilly thing which hasn't done me any favours. I'd just think I don't want to be the same as everyone else, so I wanted to have a haircut that was different, it was a bad decision".

The band ended up falling apart as Woodie explains: "There was nothing much happening it just didn't feel like it was going anywhere. It had lost its original focus. I think as Bart Coles (co singer and guitarist) had moved back to Bath. I do remember the last gig we did as The Escalators was at St Albans, it was like a garage all dayer and the guys on the p.a. were getting really uptight about how their equipment was being used and they said if anyone else drops a microphone we will turn the pa off and that's what happened somebody did drop a mic and they turned the p.a. off and we were due to be on last".

With Bart gone, Woodie explains: "The rest of us just started a band without him. The start of The Tall Boys was quite exciting and the first gig that we played was at Dingwalls. I became guitarist in The Tall Boys by default as I was guitarist in The Escalators and Nigel moved to bass to start off with and Mark Robertson played drums. We played some good gigs, but I think there is this whole thing about my stage presence as a guitarist and also the haircut, Mark just couldn't take it, I mean it was crap. There are photos of Escalators gigs where Nick Garrard gave me a hat to wear. I was sacked".

A while later Woodie joined Nigel again in The Johnson Family: "I did that for a few years, I think we started about 1988 we played on and off and by 1993 I was getting more into production". Which is where we leave Woodie's fascinating story and insights from those early heady, exciting days.

Frenzy.

One band that should have been interviewed by The Crazed was Frenzy, I used to speak to Steve Whitehouse on the telephone and remember one particular time that he told me that the rest of the band were around his house choosing the setlist for their next Klub Foot appearance. Frenzy rose to become one of the top bands at the Klub Foot. Their two classic albums Hall of Mirrors and Clockwork Toy were highly influential, and Steve was never shy to experiment with their sound adding synths to a cover of Love is the Drug by Roxy Music on Clockwork Toy. Things went a bit awry when the band released their third album Sally's Pink Bedroom which exposed their influences and ambitions ever further, cover versions of songs by Bryan Adams and Gary Numan with a slick production were a little too much for a lot of their audience. I can never understand why an interview with the band for The Crazed was never conducted, but finally after all these years here is the Frenzy/Steve Whitehouse interview.

It takes a while to finally pin Steve Whitehouse down to make the time for an interview, not that he doesn't want to do it he just seems to live in a busy, chaotic world. Due to modern technology, I didn't have to venture anywhere to conduct the interview it was through Zoom with us both sitting by our computer screens. Steve is a very angry political person and before I could ask a question he started ranting about the: "World overlords, they control everything", I couldn't stop him, finally he eventually settled: "Sorry about that had to have a little rant". A smile soon emerged back onto his face and his pride for Frenzy started coming through. "I See Red went up to number three in the indie singles chart and we stayed in the top thirty for thirty-six weeks, we stayed in the top ten for four weeks, I think. We were getting quite a bit of Radio One airplay, and we were above bands like Depeche Mode and The Smiths which was gratifying to see, I was so proud of that. Clockwork Toy the album tapped out at number eight and that stayed in for eighteen weeks in the indie top thirty".

From an early age Steve was aware of music: "My old man was Teddy Boyish and he loved Elvis, Bill Haley particularly. I was always enamoured by the slap bass sound, at five years old I said to my old man 'what's that sound? Dad, I'm going to do that one day. I got my first bass at thirteen years old called Horace". Later, Steve states he: "Was well into Matchbox and Whirlwind but I wasn't digging the Teddy Boy scene and then I saw The Stray Cats Runaway Boys on Top of the Pops and that's what influenced me. It had nothing to do with The Cramps, I didn't even know who they were. The thing that really changed me was when The Polecats came onto the scene when I saw John I'm Only Dancing on Top of the Pops, you could hear a thud when my chin hit the floor. After I immediately bought The Blue Cats Fight Back album and then the Restless album Why Don't You Just Rock, Polecats Are Go, The Deltas Boogie Disease and The Rockats Live at The Ritz they're my influences. I never liked the Psychobilly side of it and didn't overly enjoy the direction all that Grungy, Punky, Gorey Coffin stuff that never, ever did anything for me". Steve does throw in a non-rockin' influence: "Bing Crosby is probably my all-time favourite artist".

It didn't take long for Steve to start playing in a band The Shakin' Quiffs who soon caught the attention of Nervous Records supremo Roy Williams who wanted to record the band for a compilation album called Stack A Records, as Steve explains: "We did the recording for The Shakin' Quiffs in the six weeks holiday after we left school. We got dropped off at Bath Spa Station and I had the school double bass Horace which I've still got, I bought it off the school. I put Horace on its side in the cargo carriage in the train and it braked suddenly, and the bass fell on its front and split the bridge in two, I couldn't believe it, this is my big break into the music industry. I got off the train in tears. Roy Williams and Stuart Wester of Nervous Records were at Paddington Station I said to them I don't know what I'm going to do, and Roy said, 'I've got a plan' and he fucked off to a pay phone and came back and said 'it's all sorted'. We turn up at Pathway Studios and Sam Sardi (from The Ricochets) is waiting outside with his double bass and I couldn't play it. In the end they left me and Sam for an hour, then I got used to playing it". Steve also learnt how to triple slap from Sam: "All of my career to do with the slapping I'm known for is down to Sam Sardi".

Steve's ambition to get on within the music industry next came from a television show he watched: "I was watching a local music television show called RPM and there was a band on there called I think The Dixie Rebels and the front man looked really cool, had a cool guitar, good vocals and he looked the part. The drummer and bass player looked like insurance salesmen with centre partings. So, I phoned the tv studio and said could I have the telephone number of the guy who was in The Dixie Rebels, they said we can't give out telephone numbers, so I said could you tell him I am in a band, and we have the solid potential to become a good group together. A couple of days later I had a phone call from Alan Wilson the cool looking singer, he said could you do me a favour and record yourself playing slap bass in front of your stereo, so I did. He phoned me back and said this is something that's got to happen". Alan ran a music shop in Poulton and asked Steve to go over for a jam session. "We set up in the shop and it was going so well we phoned up Roy Williams and I said The Shakin' Quiffs don't exist anymore, but I've got this going and I put the phone down on the counter of the shop and we played. By the time I got back to the phone Roy was screaming down the phone 'that's amazing, record some stuff and send it up to me". So, the legendary band The Sharks were born.

The band recorded an album Phantom Rockers, but all was not well within the band as Steve explains: "We recorded the whole album and it when it came out it was all falling apart. Alan had a massive ego like I did and we clashed all the time. It wasn't like it to start with, but it ended up so volatile. We got asked to do Dutch Radio which eventually got released on the First and Last album. It was such a nightmare trip, we ended up literally in fisticuffs on the boat coming home and I'd already started Frenzy and I just said to him Fuck you I've got my own band and I don't want to see any of you again and that was it, I left the band".

Simon Brand who later formed Torment next enters Steve's journey: "Me and Gavin or Hodge (Sharks drummer) went to a music shop in Bristol because there were double basses in there and you would always go in with the pretence of being able to afford one. Simon was in there one day, I must have been fourteen and he was playing in a band called The Firebirds but he was not happy, Simon was sick of it". Before forming Frenzy, Steve and Simon had: "Already recorded a demo version of Everybody Moving and Cry or Die and we were calling ourselves Hellfire. I played drums on it and it was just me and

Simon. I sent that demo to Roy Williams and said I'm not in The Sharks anymore and he said, 'I really like that, I'll sign you for an album deal'. Merv Pepler was the drummer in a band called Suicide (not the famous New York duo). I phoned him up and I said can you play drums, come and join my band and he did". So, after a name change Frenzy was born.

Steve explains the rationale behind Frenzy: "I wanted to do stuff that was thoughtful, intelligent, I don't mean other stuff isn't intelligent. Going down the Rock route I like something with melody to it, I like chorus hooks. A lot of Frenzy stuff has big chorus hooks. We were influenced by bands like Wall of Voodoo and more Rock stuff. Who wants to be in a band doing another version of Rockin' in my Coffin". Although Frenzy did records songs with the titles Ghost Train and Skeleton Rock: "But that was tongue in cheek, the reason is that I like vintage fairgrounds I used to love going to Steam fairs with a vintage Hall of Mirrors, I used to find that cool and creepy. That's where Ghost Train comes from it's not from that horror genre it's more fun fair stuff. I own vintage fun fair stuff. When the horror thing became so serious in our scene, I thought fuck that I'm going in a different direction that's not my thing at all. We've always wanted to be different; I don't want to be the same as all the others. I don't mind being slagged off, I really don't care". Steve explains the Psychobilly label that can sometimes follow Frenzy around: "Neo Rockabilly not Psychobilly that is what I am. I play to Psychobilly audiences and I love them, I love the people, it is one of the most friendly scenes around but I am not a Psychobilly I am a Neo Rockabilly and I still think Frenzy is a Neo Rockabilly band".

After releasing the Robot Riot e.p. Frenzy set about recording their first album Hall of Mirrors for Nervous Records, but unfortunately Simon Brand left the group: "Simon Brand was creative, unfortunately because of his issues was too difficult to work with, it became apparent we were clashing. Then we drafted in Kev Saunders, his first gig was March 1984. Kev was a creative guy as well. The Hall of Mirrors album was fantastic I felt totally unchained from all the bollocks of The Sharks. We got very big because Hall of Mirrors came out and we were asked to play the Klub Foot by John Curd. Our claim to fame is we never ever opened at the Klub Foot, the lowest we were was second on the bill. Then we recorded Clockwork Toy that is a proud moment for me and I See Red".

The band were playing successful exciting gigs and the records were entering the UK indie charts. Clockwork Toy was released on ID Records and produced by Pete Gage who had previously produced Wreckin' Crew by The Meteors and who was well known throughout the music industry. The next album would see a change in fortunes for the band, who were not happy with ID Records: "When Sally's Pink Bedroom came out, that was done as a middle finger to ID Records. It was a five-album deal, we had to do one album to get out of the deal. A lot of stuff had been written to do a Frenzy style album, but we thought fuck it let's do some stuff to prove we can do stuff outside our genre and to spend as much of that record company's money as possible and make it so far out for what Frenzy is known for they won't release it, but they did. It was produced by Pat Collier who produced all the massive Katrina and The Waves hits". Steve adds: "We were going to record that material as a band called Blue Ice". Although the album might not have been recorded within the happiest of circumstances, Steve states: "We were very proud of Sally's Pink Bedroom because it shows what we could do outside the genre. It was obviously a terrible reaction to it because we were shocked when we knew it was going to be released". The bands agents started booking them as support for bands outside the Psychobilly/Rockabilly scene. "We thought we could break out of the genre and make more of a long-lasting career. The Rockabilly/Psychobilly thing is like a bubble and the surface tension will never let you get out, the occasional band has done, you've got to have money, luck and power behind you for that to happen. We thought Sally's Pink Bedroom would be that record to break us out and get us on some of those different genre tours but the momentum outside of our scene never took over enough for it to snowball into anything better". In conclusion Steve adds: "So we got stuck with an album that most Rockabilly's/Psychobilly's hated. I still love it, it isn't Frenzy, really it is just self-indulgence at the record company's expense. I do apologise". The fall out led Steve to: "Take a year off 1988, the band didn't exist, Kev parted ways and he never came back to the band. When I came back, we recorded the This is the Fire album". Steve has continued to tour and release records with Frenzy including the brilliant In The Blood album, his enthusiasm, excitement and determination has never diminished.

You would imagine the story would end there but Steve ended up joining two of the biggest Neo Rockabilly bands ever, Restless and The Blue Cats. Steve explains: "I joined Restless in 1990, not a lot of people know this but Restless had split up by that point because Jeff Bayly had left the band because of his lorry driving. I had a letter from Pete Gage Productions stating that I'd been invited to accompany Restless as the bass player on their tour of Japan. I phoned him up and said yeah, I know all the material. We did three gigs, that was a five-year career. Unfortunately, it fell apart in Japan because I organised a tour of Frenzy and Restless together and I was playing twice a night, Frenzy were supporting Restless, it was a really good tour. We went to an in-store record signing it was meant to be for both bands and I arranged it to be for both bands but when I got there it was only Frenzy stuff that had been put up and I don't know why. We were at the Dublin Castle in Camden not long afterwards and Mark (Harman) said to me you're going to have to make a decision it's either Frenzy or Restless you can't do both. I didn't make that decision then we did a gig in Sweden and I was sat in Antwerp having a meal and he said you haven't made the decision I'm making the decision for you, last night was the last gig. We're best of friends now".

Steve's involvement with The Blue Cats: "I've always been a massive fan, they asked me to join in 2011. I came home from work one day and my missus says to me I think you better listen to the answerphone there's something on there you might like, so I listened to it Clint (the singer) just said 'Steve it's Clint Bradley here from The Blue Cats we're getting it all back together, just wondered if you want to be part of The Blue Cats. I couldn't pick the phone up fast enough, we were chatting for three hours, my missus kept coming up to the room rolling her eyes. I couldn't believe my luck. It was just like we had always played together. When we finished the last song of the set everybody was beaming ear to ear and I'll never forget Clint put his guitar down, he came over to me and gave me a massive man hug and said, 'you should have joined the band years ago'. What an accolade, I couldn't believe what I was hearing" Steve is also: "The official reserve bass player for The Polecats when Phil can't do it". He finishes: "If you're a fan boy you will always be even if you are in a band".

Glenn Daeche.

I was in the Bear Pub in Northampton on the first night of the Bedlam Psychobilly Festival in 2022 enjoying the party atmosphere. After two years of lockdown everyone seemed to be reconnecting and enjoying the lively atmosphere that was being generated. Beer was flowing, the laughing and chatting was getting louder, a good time was being had by all. Old friendships were being rekindled and new ones being made. I was soaking this all in and loving every minute of it, although nothing could replace the old days of the Klub Foot this was as close it was going to get. As I walked through the pub trying desperately not to spill my pint, I spotted Glenn Daeche singer and guitarist from The Pharaohs who I had interviewed a few months back for this book. I went over and had a chat Glenn who was as chatty and friendly as he was during my Zoom interview with him. I had the idea of taking a photo of him for the book, but Glenn remembering my complimentary comments about his band suggested recording a short clip to upload onto my phone, my wife Dawn took my phone and started filming whilst Glenn asked me: "The best underrated band ever?", as I had a few pints this did not completely filter into my brain correctly: "One of the best songwriters on the scene without a doubt, Glenn from The Pharaohs", "Ok I'll take that" he answered. Of course, The Pharaohs were very underrated and should have been much bigger within the scene. They were certainly one of the highlights on Stomping at the Klub Foot Volume Two and Blue Egypt remains a popular album even after all these years.

The following interview was undertaken using Zoom, with Glenn in his living room and me in mine. If it wasn't for the Pandemic, I would not have been aware of Zoom but here was Glenn appearing on my computer monitor: "It's unreal" he commented before the interview was due to start. Who would have thought in the eighties that many years later an interview could be conducted like this.

The first question I asked was how did Glenn get into the rockin' scene? "I started out as a Teddy Boy and I went to a Rock 'n' Roll club in Bishops Stortford for about five to six years and it was great at first and then after a few years I thought Teddy Boys have got a tunnel vision, all rules and regulations on what you should like. All the original Teddy Boys looked at the young guy's as plastic Teds and I didn't like that. I thought they looked stupid in drainpipe trousers and great big brothel creepers. Then the DJ at HoundDogs (a rockin' club) started playing all this imported Rockabilly music. He started playing all this obscure Rockabilly and what came with Rockabilly was the fashion like pegged trousers and flat top haircuts. I thought this is where I want to go down".

Glenn also wanted to get more involved with the scene instead of just attending Rockabilly nights at the club: "I remember going into the toilets having a wee and you get brilliant acoustics in the toilet with the echo, and I was singing Honey Don't while I was having a piss and I thought that doesn't sound bad. So, that's what influenced me into starting a band". The band were originally called The Phantom Pharaohs. "First gig was at HoundDogs Rock 'n' Roll club on 10th April 1982. I remember that clearly because I got done for drinking and driving at the end of it". Were the early gigs mostly full of covers? "It was about half and half; we didn't want to play Rockabilly/Rock 'n' Roll covers. The idea of having a new band is to have new ideas, if you are going to do covers don't do them like the originals which I don't think we did. I can only do my own interpretation of it. If you are that good at doing something do your own stuff. The covers are just to fill up a set list if you're doing a gig for forty-five minutes. I think we all did that in the early days". He also adds: "We didn't want to do Elvis Presley, we don't want carbon copies of the original rockin' bands because a lot of bands were doing that in the early eighties, and they were doing it well, but to me I couldn't see the point of that because we're here and now. What's the point of digging up something, you might as well get a Johnny Burnette album and play it because you ain't going to get better than that".

Another big influence on Glenn before the band played their first gig were The Meteors: "I first saw The Meteors in '81 and they blew me away and I will never forget those early days. People might have their opinions about The Meteors but what they did for the music, if it wasn't for them, we wouldn't all be doing this, we would all be like Matchbox and Flying Saucers and playing covers in pubs. The Pharaohs you wouldn't think would sound like The Meteors, but you don't have to sound like them to be influenced, take something and put your spin on it". Glenn shares his opinions on the Rockabilly/Psychobilly scenes: "I always look at this from two angles, the Psychobilly scene itself it all started off we were all into Rockabilly bands doing Carl Perkins, Roy Orbison Rockhouse and all those types of things. You get the other section the Psychobilly half that comes from the Punk side of stuff. So, you had two channels and I think the majority of the early rockin' bands come from that Elvis, Buddy Holly influence and buying those albums. I remember MCA Rare Rockabilly, there's three of them and I was like whoa and this was classed as Rockabilly". Glenn adds: "I used to hate Punk bands when I was a Teddy Boy, we didn't get on with Punks. We were young and stupid and didn't understand it all. Now I listen to The Sex Pistols and love it, but I wasn't brought up on that stuff". The double bass also proved to be a novelty for those early gig goers. "I remember when you did gigs and you had the double bass on stage and when people would come in and look at the double bass, it didn't matter what anyone else was doing". The early Pharaohs also had a guitarist who wasn't a Rockabilly: "The lead guitarist wasn't Rockabilly at all, he was a bit more like Jimi Hendrix". Although Glenn states: "As long as I had the original Rockabilly thing which is the theme the band forms around what I do". He then adds laughing: "We had a double bass player what more do you want, as far as Rockabilly's concerned". Although Glenn adds: "Our double bass player stopped playing 'cos he met a girlfriend and didn't want to do it anymore and we ended up getting Lee Brown on electric bass".

The Pharaohs soon picked up a healthy local following within the Harlow area, this led to gigs in London and a record deal with Nervous Records as Glenn explains: "We got this gig at The Clarendon which is the downstairs bar at The Klub Foot supporting The Rapids and we brought two fifty-seater coaches from Harlow, where we come from. The place had a hundred in there who were all Pharaohs supporters and no one for The Rapids. John Curd (who ran The Klub Foot) looked out of the window as it was also a Klub Foot night and he thought where did those two coaches come from? Who are they? Someone said it's The Pharaohs. So, we actually got our foot in the door not because we were any good but by the fact, he (John Curd) saw a hundred people going to the downstairs bar and that's how we got into The Klub Foot. I think that's the gig Roy Williams (from Nervous Records) turned up at, he just came up to me and said do you want to do a record deal? Yeah of course".

Just before Nervous Records released the bands Blue Egypt album the band had two tracks featured on the Stomping at The Klub Foot Volume Two album. The two tracks showed a confident and powerful sounding band and still remain two of the best tracks recorded from those classic nights. "They're the only two I do guitar solos on". Glenn's opinion of the Blue Egypt isn't quite as complimentary though: "I thought the album was rubbish, the way it was recorded there was hardly any bass, we enhanced the bass of Becker's bass drum to get more bass in the songs. If you compare the stuff on Blue Egypt to the live stuff at the Klub Foot, you would think we were two different bands. There was an £8000.00 budget to do that album, you used to make money in those days, only a little bit, you don't make money now. One night we all went home the producer Doc Stewart came in with some electric drums and thought that sounds good and went through the whole album, I thought no. The strange thing is that sold more albums than any of the other albums put together, which is ridiculous. The only one I think is any good on that album is Killed Love". Many years later The Pharaohs re-recorded some of the songs for an album called Blue Egyptian. "I didn't think it represented those good songs properly, so that's why I revamped half the songs. It is not a reproduction of Blue Egypt, half is, they've been done better in my view". Glenn also doesn't believe the album helped much in promoting the band back then: "I think the popularity in the early days came from the two tracks on Stomping. Especially abroad like Germany. That came from Stomping and not being on Nervous Records". One of the songs from the album was featured on Channel Four's Come Dine with Me TV show "Blue Egypt's on it" Glenn proudly states.

The Pharaohs became a regular band at the Klub Foot. "The Pharaohs never got better than second headline, but everyone thinks we're this big Klub Foot band although we are one of the pioneers of the bands who played at the Klub Foot". Glenn goes on to describe the Klub Foot: "It had condensation coming down the side of the walls and it was all mouldy and smelly. It was iconic, never to be done again, it had its own personality, it's something to do with the venue and the time. Drinking cans of Skol that's what it was all about. Anyone who has ever played there has a piece of history". He also adds: "We are the only Rockabilly band to have played Rockabilly and Punk nights".

The band followed up Blue Egypt with a twelve-inch ep Vigilante which Glenn is very proud of: "If you play that now it sounds like it was recorded yesterday, it was way ahead of its time but it's all too late, it's all water under the bridge now but I'm proud of that we tried to do a twelve-inch single for a wider audience". The band also released the Hammer & Sickel Blues album, which was also released on Nervous Records, Glenn discusses the album: "I loved the cover. That was the album where we took note of what other people were doing, it's a slight cop out as it was The Pharaohs trying to be a Psychobilly band. My favourite track is Crazy Crazy Happenings it's pretty Psychobilly and I think it's a good rendition of a Psychobilly song. Drumming's fantastic and the bass playing is fast but not all in tune". There was a slightly controversial song on it called Psycho Numbskull which did not have the most complimentary lyrics regarding the Klub Foot, Glenn attempts to explain: "It was why are Psychobilly bands more successful than me. I'm a Rockabilly band but it was tongue in cheek, and we were famous for not ever, ever being allowed to play on a Meteors gig ever again even though I gave him (P Paul Fenech) my bass player Lee Brown, although I took it as a compliment as at least he listened to it". Glenn explains how The Pharaohs electric bass player Lee Brown left the band to join The Meteors: "We were at the Klub Foot and The Meteors bass player didn't turn up and our bass player Lee Brown was a Meteors fanatic, and he knew all the songs. We said to him go on up there and he actually joined the band that night but didn't play, someone else did. I felt good about that". After the release of the album in 1988 The Pharaohs didn't release another record until 2000, Glenn states: "The Pharaohs got stuck in the nineties and didn't really move on".

Glenn shares his opinion about the Psychobilly scene: "There are egos but at the end of the day the camaraderie between all the bands is brilliant. I enjoy going to gigs as much as playing them. The

Pharaohs are part of the history which I think they are an important little piece of the jigsaw that makes up the whole genre, I'm proud to be part of that. A bit of me is a bit sour because we should have been bigger than what we were but a lot of that is down to me not being pushy enough. I'm not a businessman, I write good songs, I'm not a very good front man. If you can write a song with a melody and still have a vibe with it, then you have the answer. The way I write songs I like melody and Psychobilly is more about a vibe rather than a song with a melody in it. My most influential artist is Buddy Holly; I love Buddy Holly the man writes melody". He then describes his vision for the future: "You got to have all these genres (Rockabilly/Psychobilly) together, we should all get together and become one big scene, and everyone will start making money".

You certainly can't argue with Glenn's last observation regarding bands with different styles within the rockin' scene joining up and coexisting to make it much larger and financially viable. The Pharaohs do deserve much more recognition for their contribution to the scene and Glenn remains one of the most underrated song writers. He did however receive some recognition during lockdown when he broadcast a popular one man show on Facebook featuring him and his guitar skilfully belting out songs. "I'm more popular in lockdown than I ever was" he said at the time.

Red Hot Riot.

I saw this band two nights in a row during 2022 when they played in Kent, once in The Chambers in Folkestone and the following night at The Anchor in Wingham. They were great in The Chambers but absolutely smashed the evening at The Anchor. The excitement and energy the band generated throughout their performance was infectious and exciting to see and hear. For a new, young band to play their own version of this style of music with so much passion was exhilarating and showed that the scene was not slipping into nostalgia and was moving excitingly forwards. The band had already released an album on Western Star Records entitled Forget Me Not, but what they played live was much more powerful than the sound captured on that album. In my excitement of witnessing these two powerhouse performances I approached the band for an interview for this book and soon became aware that they were not fully aware of how great those gigs were (although I'm sure after my raving, they might have had an inclining). Ricky Delaney, singer and guitarist for the band agreed to an interview and it was left that it would be arranged for when they were due to play at the Bedlam Festival in Northampton.

On the last day of a fantastic Bedlam Festival, Ricky and Louis Barnett (the bands other guitarist) were in The Roadmender venue at Bedlam. I was there with my wife Dawn and received a message on my phone: "Hi mate, we're at Bedlam now, me and Louis can do the interview whenever you're ready". It didn't take me too long to spot the rather tall Ricky at the venue, walk over and say: "Let's go". The only problem for me was that the venue was busy and there was nowhere suitable to conduct the interview. I made the decision to take the two members of the band around the side of the venue and undertake the interview there, forgetting that it would also pick up road noise and punters walking into the venue on the small microphone of my voice recorder.

Ricky and Louis were just as friendly and approachable as they were when I met them in Kent, both seemed keen to be interviewed and showed an understanding and patience whilst I tried to clear the alcohol induced fog out of my brain to start the interview. I had decided not to have any questions written and to try a free-flowing conversational interview. Hope it worked.

Why would a group of young lads decide to form a rockin' band? I can understand why so many bands were formed back in the day, what with the Klub Foot etc but today the rockin' climate is different. There is a strong element of nostalgia for those old wreckin' days. The spirit is still there even if the outward appearance is now greyer, chubbier with thinning or long-gone quiffs replaced by shining bald domes. Ricky explains his motivation: "Myself and the bass player (Scott McParland), we were in another band, but it was garage like The Sonics and stuff like that and we were struggling to get gigs. Scott could play double bass, so we thought why not do a Rockabilly gig as a one off to make a bit of extra money, because we like Rockabilly, Psychobilly and Rock 'n' Roll. So, we did it as a one-off gig, that was all it was going to be, a bit of fun, but we enjoyed it that much we'd do it a bit more and it started from there really. We were a three piece for eighteen months then Louis joined us a four piece". Why did you recruit Louis as a second guitarist? Ricky: "We recorded the album at Western Star and I did a lot of extra guitar work on top of it and we wanted to recreate it live. I wouldn't go back to a three piece". Louis explains why: "It fills it out". Ricky: "Live we are a lot heavier than we are on record. We have heard people say there is a contrast between the album and live". That is certainly true, any preconceived ideas about the band taken from listening to the album are blown away once the band are heard in their true setting on stage. The songs take on a power that is not always evident on Forget Me Not. Louis: "It is hard to recreate that onto an album. Blackbird (a new song at the time) captures that the best at the moment. It was trying to capture that energy of our live performance into a studio recording".

The band draw their sound from many different influences. Ricky explains that he grew up in a rockin' household: "My grandparents were strong blooded Teds. My mum is very neo–Rockabilly, The Stray Cats and The Polecats and my dad's more Psychobilly and Punk. So, those all came together, and I had no choice really. I wouldn't have it any other way, I love it. I love modern Indie bands,

Punk, Green Day, I like Bad Religion". Louis: "I like late forties, early fifties, I like the old stuff, that genre. I'm rooted quite strongly into the Rockabilly stuff. I do like the newer stuff, but I do like the older stuff that's where my musical roots are. Sonny Burgess, Elvis is my idol". By joining the band Louis explains: "There's a whole other side of it I hadn't heard, the band are broadening my horizon". Ricky mentioned The Stray Cats some people have compared the band to them, Louis: "That's amazing that". Ricky: "I've got a Stray Cats tattoo". Louis: "They made a massive impact". Ricky: "I love The Stray Cats, I know they are a bit of a Marmite band, some people either love them or hate them but at the end of the day it's good music. So, who cares if it got in the charts or not? They are a great band in my opinion".

Do the band find it restrictive being a band within the Rockabilly/Psychobilly scene? Louis: "It's quite a niche market". Ricky: "It labels you a certain style and people get an image in their heads, but if you can win them over, like us doing Glastonbury and the commercial side of stuff. You can get into those things and then I think you really do stand out. How many bands doing commercial gigs use a double bass? That really does help out". Are Red Hot Riot trying to take it forward? "We're trying to". Louis: "That's what people like us for". Ricky: "Because we're not stuck, we've got an incentive to work with different things. We can branch out". But will it always have a rockin' influence? "Louis: "Oh yes, we've kind of got our own thing going". Ricky: "If we get the Rockabilly's and Psychobilly's on side, they're so loyal". Louis: "Psychobilly bands are very nice people, very welcoming and you can have great fun. It makes it all worthwhile". Louis also adds: "We're playing Las Vegas and Pineda as well". How do the band fit within the Rockabilly and Psychobilly scenes? Louis: "We are like borderline in the middle with it, it kind of works". Ricky: " I like Restless, I listen to the Rockabilly and Psychobilly stuff. I like to be able to play both. I like playing both the Psychobilly and Rockabilly festivals". Do the ages of the audiences vary much? Louis: "Certain places there is an older generation and others there's younger, depends on where we go really".

Alan Wilson's Western Star Records released the band's debut album Forget Me Not, how did that come about? Ricky: "He (Alan Wilson) saw us online and got in touch and it went from there really. Alan heard it and said he liked it and he contacted us and said I want to record you guys and then we played at a Rockabilly fair and met him. It was a no brainer really". Were you happy with the results? Ricky: "Yeah, we were trying to capture all the live element on it. We are a live band anyway; we prefer playing live to recording. I think recording is just part of everything". Louis: "Good fun, all good fun". You stated Alan Wilson discovered the band online, what is your opinion of social media? Ricky: "I think social media is the way forward, it has pros and cons really. Anyone can get themselves out there but on the same hand anyone can do it, so much out there. It becomes very condensed trying to find new bands, how they promote themselves". What about Spotify? Which is always a contentious issue amongst musicians. Ricky: "We have to do it. I mean I do like vinyl but when I'm driving the car I put on my Spotify as I'm not having a record player everywhere I go, so, Spotify's the equal for that". Louis: "You discover a lot on it, hopefully we are being discovered on it". The Crazed's good friend Bracko suddenly appears and makes his presence known, the band laugh not quite realising he is the author of the brilliant Hell's Bent on Rockin', a chirpy Bracko walks off into the distance.

Ricky explains that he is the main song writer within the band: "The other guys do their own bit, but it definitely holds from my original idea". Louis: "We all have ideas and try and see what works, from the demo to the actual recording it's completely different, it develops along the way". Ricky: "I don't try to put a restraint on my writing and the other guys come into it and add their own styles and it becomes Red Hot Riot". The band also include a cracking version of the old Stray Cats classic Rock This Town into their live performances, Ricky explains: "We have a play about and just do our own version, every gig we just jam it out in the middle, its good fun, I like that there's no restrictions on what we're doing with it, it's our own thing every gig".

What is the end plan for the band? Louis: "We haven't really got an end plan apart from keep on going. Every step up now we're getting better and better and everything's falling into place. We've just got to keep doing what we're doing". Ricky: "It will be nice to reach the point where we don't have to sleep in the van every night and to sleep in a hotel bed, that's where I want to be". He explains that presently: "We literally have a bed in the back of the van". Louis: "We all work full time, it's quite a demanding thing being in a band but it's worth it. We all get on really well which is a bonus". Ricky: " If we weren't in a band, we would be meeting up at the weekend anyway".

On that very pleasant note the interview concludes, we all head back into the Bedlam Festival with Red Hot Riot due to play the nearby Bear Pub later that evening. The band are without any doubt one of the most exciting lives acts around and are a band not afraid to expand their influences outside the sometimes claustrophobic and stifling rockin' scene. I am really excited where their journey takes them next.

The Defiant Ones.

What happens when the teenage enthusiasm that you had for the Rockabilly/Psychobilly scene doesn't go, you are still infected with the rockin' disease and those doors of the Klub Foot that closed permanently so many years ago and were physically destroyed are still wide open in your mind. Those Earwigs are still in your Brain and it is still Raining in Pittsburgh. Why you would most likely form a band with a group of likeminded lost souls and name yourselves The Defiant Ones! Which is exactly what Marcus Heywood did in January 2019. Marcus as you may remember from earlier in the book was present during my interview with The Caravans outside Dingwalls in Camden Town. We used to hang out with the same rockin' people during the eighties spending many a moment pondering life over a lukewarm cup of tea within some tired looking café. Now he is singing and howling for this band.

The following interview was conducted a week before their appearance at the Bedlam Psychobilly Festival in Northampton. The band were in good spirits at Good Rehearsal Studios in Manston, Kent which impressively has a bar. I tried to initially start the interview in the bar, but it seemed impossible due to all five members of the band deciding to scatter themselves around and not really paying proper attention to my feeble requests to start the interview. Fortunately, it was decided to undertake the interview in one of the rehearsal rooms that was free, where we quickly reconvened in a very comfortable, spacious room and with the band now paying full attention the interview was conducted.

If you stare at your original Stomping at the Klub Foot album covers, you may be able to spot two members of the band within the crowd. Marcus was on the cover of volume three and also appeared in the video of that legendary night sticking his finger up a friend's nose whilst being filmed waiting outside the venue. Bass slapper Soap was on the back cover of the classic first album of the series, although guitarist Tony was also there but narrowly missed being featured on the cover, as Soap explains: "I got that album as we were there, and he (Tony) buggered off to the bar. I went to his house and said that the Klub Foot album's out, I handed it to him, and he went you bastard". Tony: "I had buggered off to the bar". What a time to get your round in! Soap: "The Klub Foot was the mecca and once that had gone......". Marcus: "I was there all the time". Although Marcus stayed heavily into the scene Soap tended to move away and veer towards the garage bands such as The Sting-Rays, The X-Men and The Vibes who later morphed into The Purple Things. Soap explains why and his view on some of the bands that followed: "I always found that to be all slap and nothing else and I like what came before that on that scene. I think a lot of bands that followed didn't appeal to me, maybe the odd songs". Tony explains his introduction: "When I was thirteen, I loved The Who, I never heard of Rockabilly didn't know what it was, when I first heard (The Cramps) Human Fly there was no drug that made me feel that good". When he saw them: "In Brixton I stood there open mouthed, I hadn't had a drink and there's been nothing like that ever. I love good Rock 'n' Roll". Once bitten the rockin' fever never stopped infecting Tony just like the rest of the band.

Marcus explains the original idea behind starting the band: "When we originally started the idea was we were going to do songs by The Cramps and The Meteors, covers. Then when we started writing our own and that eighties influence has come out in the writing and the music really". Was it intentional? "Marcus: "No, it's not intentional but it's where we are all based, it's our background and it just sort of came about, we didn't set up to go we're going to do the eighties, but that sound comes because it's what we're all into. Once we started writing I remember Soap saying to me that with the band going in the direction we're in now there's going to be a load of old Scooter boys, old Punks and old Psychobilly's who are going to like this because we like it and that is its appeal".

The main songwriters in the band are mainly Marcus and Soap. Marcus explains his contribution: "Definitely, lyric wise, everyone else - Tony does the guitar. Peck sorts out more the arranging side of things and as everyone's involved it sounds different than it originally did in my head". Soap: "If I have an idea for a song and I've got the chords you've got it in your head, but once everyone's joined in, it becomes something else, ninety times out of a hundred it's better rather than a one-dimensional song". Soap also mentions one of the pitfalls of song writing: "Sometimes you end up writing things that sound very similar". Drummer Peck chips in: "You got to do what you believe in, otherwise it's just another twelve bar". Marcus: "We try to keep away from Cadillacs and Trains". Soap: "You get really bored with that". Marcus mentions a couple of Defiant Ones songs that go down a different route: "Anxiety, Pre-Occupied, we do different subjects". Apart from the obvious Psychobilly and Rockabilly influences Marcus explains the band also like: "Glam Rock as well, Marc Bolan". Soap: "And of course Punk Rock. We could either try and be an authentic Rockabilly band or do something that's original". Marcus: "We could do a song and if it came out like Dexy's Midnight Runners, but we liked it we'll play it". Marcus: "Sometimes when we do a song it might have a Restless sound or a Meteors sound in our heads, but something comes out and you make it your own and don't be scared if it ain't Rockabilly". Tony then explains his guitar style as: "Mutant Cochran". Marcus: "Rather than say we are Rockabilly or Psychobilly I would say we are a Klub Foot band, it's a good thing".

The band got a deal with TrashWax Records who at the time of writing had released their debut album Savage Songs from The Teen-Age Jungle which featured an excellent selection of songs including the bands classic The TV Has Stolen My Brain! Marcus explains how difficult it was to get noticed by record companies: "I was pushing us and got turned down by lots of people, some didn't even want to listen to us. I then got in touch with a friend of mine in France who got in touch with Darren Crane of TrashWax who liked what we did and said we'd give it a go, so, we recorded it (the album). Peck mastered it, then it came out. Three weeks later Soap came round with the hump saying what's happened? they're not advertising our record anymore, I said it's because it's sold out". Marcus then slightly bitterly states: "There are some people selling our record now who turned us down". The album had a lo fi sound, Soap: "It's not deliberately lo fi". Peck: "I know what I want to hear and I'll put the mics where I want them to be and we won't worry too much about bleeds and all that kind of stuff, the productions just about the song. I would like to have a bit more control over Marcus's vocals". Soap: "If you turn him up it creates the electricity or intensity". When it came to writing and recording the songs Soap explains: "When we recorded the album it was during lockdown, like we had three songs, we would go in and record them and then when we came to play them live, we better actually learn them". Marcus: "Sometimes me and Soap would bring a song along and do it in a couple of takes, then we never bloody remembered it". Did you have to make the lyrics up when you preformed the songs live? Marcus: "We had them all written down and it was like how does that go? And that's why sometimes it doesn't actually sound like the record". Peck: "We're not a professional band of musicians, we don't want it to be note perfect, we want it to have energy over technical ability, we like to listen to things that move you. One of the signature recording techniques I use, I let everything bleed into Marcus's microphone, that's how all the good sounds I like in Rockabilly/Psychobilly have been created". Soap: "That first Meteors ep they recorded in an old cinema and literally recorded it live and that is what we are going for". Soap also explains that: "Alan Wilson of Western Star wanted us to re-record it over five days and two days mixing". Tony jokingly adds: "It wouldn't have made us any better, it would have shown us as shoddy musicians".

Live the band are always entertaining to watch with Marcus's on-stage antics always the main focus. Peck: "I enjoy playing with Marcus, it's nice to have someone out front who doesn't give a shit. I have been in a lot of bands and a lot of singers tend to be self-aware and not wanting to make a fool of themselves, he's out there, he's with the crowd and people enjoy it". Marcus: "I always enjoy it, rolling around on the floor, I might not always be able to get up (laughs)". Peck: "When we start playing an intro and then Marcus comes out, it lifts it even more. I like a bit of theatre in the show". Marcus: "I try to be what I want to be (on stage)". Marcus then humbly turns to Soap: "I think we need a bit more of Soap's humour to come through because when we're rehearsing that comes through well".

We then all leave the rehearsal studios and the band perform at a successful Bedlam the following week and lay tracks down for their follow up album that may include a hilarious and catchy original song called Penistone which Marcus's partner Sally absolutely hates. The enthusiasm and drive The Defiant Ones have is infectious, the quiffs may be greyer or receding but the band is not allowing time to slow them down, the dusty doors of the Klub Foot are being pulled open again by them even if the physical location of the venue is gone.

Simon Crowfoot.

Always the most mysterious looking member of Torment with his huge (sometimes) red quiff and emotionless expression on stage. Simon was a member of the now legendary trio playing on classic albums like Psyclops Carnival and Three's A Crowd. The band from those early days featured in The Crazed have now gained a legendary status within the Psychobilly scene. As stated, earlier singer and guitarist Simon Brand is sadly no longer with us. The two surviving members Simon and Kevin Haynes did reform Torment with Andy Kandil respectfully taking Simon Brands role on stage. Simon Crowfoot now lives in New Zealand and agreed to be interviewed for this book, obviously a face-to-face interview was not possible, so Simon kindly answered my questions via email.

Q. A lot of people who got into Psychobilly originally listened to Rockabilly. I used to listen to those cheap Pickwick Records compilation albums which featured Sun Records artists. Did you follow a similar route?

A. Yes, I did follow a similar route. I got hooked on Rockabilly after seeing the Stray Cats in Bristol in 1981, ice and snow on the ground but still drove 25 miles to get there. Then joined a Rockabilly band from Gloucester called The Kernals and was obsessed with Rockabilly, buying a lot of records and seeing a lot of rockin' bands, until I left to join Torment.

Q. P Paul Fenech said in an interview that Rockabilly was comparable to Punk in the fifies. I agree with this opinion as I feel it was edgier and less predictable than Rock 'n' Roll. Dixie Fried by Carl Perkins and Honey Hush by Johnny Burnette are two songs that spring to mind. What is your take on this?

A. I totally agree with Paul Fenech's comment, way edgier than the almost predictable Rock 'n' Roll formula..... not to say that there are not good Rock 'n' Roll songs, there are some brilliant ones, it's just that Rockabilly had just that bit more intenseness for me. Just listen to the angst and searing guitar of Johnny Powers Long Blonde Hair for example.

Q. Music was so important to me when I was growing up as it seemed to define who I was. Did you feel the same and how did it influence you?

A. I was always listening to the 40's Jazz that my dad used to play at home and so was exposed to it from a young age. When I got into Rockabilly it did make me feel alive and was part of who I was and what I wanted to become. So proud of that that I didn't go the path of say Heavy Metal. Ha-ha. once a Rocker always a Rocker, eh?

Q. Most early Psychobilly bands state that The Meteors were a major influence.

A. I agree that in those early days of Psychobilly we used to thrash those early Meteors albums and played quite a few of those songs. In the early days of my first couple of Psychobilly bands The Cultic Heads and The Swamp Toads. So yes, a pretty big part of the initiation into Psychobilly.

Q. How did you get to join Torment and what was your initial impression?

A. Simon called me up and asked me if I wanted to join as their bass player and a good friend of mine to Tony Biggs was leaving the band. My initial impression and thoughts were that hey this could be a really good band to be in and doing some good gigs around the country and overseas with. I was impressed with what I was seeing at those early practices.

Q. When did you first meet Simon Brand

A. I first met Simon Brand after he called me up and asked me if I wanted to join Torment. We had a long talk about what and where we wanted the band to go, and we all went on developing from there.

Q. How difficult was Simon to work with, the image I have of him is of an intense and driven individual.

A. At times it was impossible to work together or see eye to eye, and at other times things flowed smoothly. He was a driven sort of a guy but sometimes that got in the way of equal band division. He was a very creative mind and a good songwriter.

Q. His death must have been devasting. Do you wish to discuss the impact?

A. I have to admit I was really stunned when I heard the news, it was after I had left the band and I was living in Amsterdam, Holland. It was something that I never thought would or could happen. even though I had heard he had had a few issues with his life and mental health, I didn't think he would have taken it that far.

Q. Due to the tragedy with Simon and the strength and quality of your records and performances, the group has entered legendary status within the Psychobilly scene, how does being part of it feel?

A. Being part of Torment for me makes me feel lucky to have had the opportunity to make music that has as times gone on still be popular in the scene some nearly 30 years on.

Q. The Klub Foot (where many interviews were held) any views/stories about the venue?

A. I feel very proud to have played there at the mecca of Psychobilly quite a few times over a few years. The first time I went there was to see The Meteors and Restless on the same bill. If my memory serves me well Restless played at one end of the hall and then The Meteors at the other. Always good times there and as we were all young it had a big impression on me. Exciting times with all those crazy cats who felt the same way I did and loved the wild music and explosive scene. I remember one night there when I saw someone coming out of the toilets with a bleeding nose saying, "The Bristol lads are here again tonight", nothing to do with me by the way. The Klub Foot was a brilliant venue, moisture running down the walls by the end of the gig and really dodgy electric wires being held up with gaffer tape high up on the walls to power the place. ha-ha.

Q. I remember once being told by a manager of one of the bands playing at the Klub Foot not to wear his bands t-shirt as they were having problems with another band on the bill. Was there a lot of rivalry between bands?

A. No, we didn't have any rivalry with other bands although I did hear a lot of stories about that going on in the scene. The rivalry thing comes down to people's ideas about who they are and what they think they stand for in the scene, their ranking and all that stuff. I didn't have a problem with anyone. As Simon wrote in Mystery Man... "Jealousy rules the crowd" although I don't think that he was alluding to rivalry between bands.

Q. When the Klub Foot closed the Psychobilly scene in the UK seemed to disintegrate, how was this period for you and Torment? Did the scene become stronger in the rest of Europe?

A. When the Klub Foot closed, I felt, and I'm sure the rest of Torment felt like it was what now? Where do we play that's as cool and important as there? The Klub Foot was the anchor for all of us for Psychobilly. Then a lot of gigs were held at the L.M.S. pub. not a patch on the Klub Foot and the gig band line-ups seemed to be not as good as those held at the Klub Foot either. The scene did become stronger in Europe at this time which was just about the time I left Torment.

Q. What did the band think of Psyclops Carnival once it was released (the production etc).

A. I remember us all thinking that the album was way too toppy and I can remember Simon and I saying it reminded us of a knitting machine going full speed. But what do you expect for 500 quid??? I think the cover photo is a brilliant one and was taken up on Clifton suspension bridge in Bristol, a legendary Bristol landmark.

Q. Your second album Threes A Crowd was produced by Steve Whitehouse. How did this come about and what did you think of the results? (The album was also the only album I ever received free from Roy Williams).

A. I think that it was an idea from Kevin Haynes to get Steve in to produce the album, then agreed on by Roy Williams. I think it was a great result and job well done by him.

Q. Didn't one of your albums (Three's A Crowd) enter the indie charts, I seem to remember seeing it listed.

A. Yes, that is correct we did enter the indie charts, probably in 1987. I can't honestly say if it was Three's a Crowd album, but I remember it was at number 17 for 2 weeks before dropping out.

Q. Apart from the Klub Foot were gigs hard to find in the UK?

A. Yes, gigs were hard to get in the UK for us but saying that we weren't playing as much as some of the other bands. and from what I remember we were doing a gig once every six weeks or something like that, which had its advantages as we didn't get bored of playing and weren't always in the public eye and so I'd say people were more likely to come and see us as it was something different than the more regularly gigging Psycho bands.

Q. Why the change of image with the Round the World album?

A. The image of Round the World album was a bit of our choice in the photo images, going a bit more greasy Rocker. The electronic drums were Roy Williams idea... I didn't like that from the start, to me it detracted from the true Psychobilly feel of the music, which I think the public also felt too.

Q. Why did you leave Torment?

A. I left Torment because I was going to move to Amsterdam, Holland to be with my girl. I said I would still do the gigs but was told that I was sacked. Hahaha. I think they had already decided on that one. It all got a bit nasty in the end after I had left, so felt it was better to not go back and do some reunion gigs a year or so after when I was asked. I just politely bowed out.

Q. Why do you think Psychobilly has never gone mainstream?

A. I think that Psychobilly has never gone mainstream because as with Punk it's a bit too wild to be played on the radio, or to be seen on TV. Or was at that time. The media didn't like Punk so why are they going to embrace Psychobilly??? and it's the underground scene like Psychobilly that makes it attractive to people, because we are different from the rest of society! It's a cool scene.

Q. Whose idea was it to reform Torment?

A. The idea to reform Torment came from Kev. I hadn't seen Kev in something like 28 years and he contacted me ...and when I went to the UK at Christmas, we met up and we chatted like old friends, picked up just where we left off. We decided to go and do this thing again for the Pineda Psychobilly Festival which was absolutely brilliant, we were so happy to have achieved that.

Q. Torment had a unique sound, how much pressure was it to live up to the fans expectations and regain that unique sound?

A. Yes Torment had a unique sound and now we are doing this with Andy who is a maestro and genius when it comes to playing and sound, the Torment sound is still there and it felt just like 1986 for us when we played in Pineda last year. I'm sure Simon Brand would have been smiling if he was listening in.

Simon continues to be a popular figure within the Psychobilly scene, his status with the legendary Torment forever etched in Psychobilly history and his contribution on Demented Are Go's In Sickness and In Health album which Simon wishes to state "I am listed as playing on Rubber Love but it's actually Frenzied Beat that I am playing on". He even started his own band within New Zealand called The Crowfoot Conspiracy which included songs by Torment and his first Psychobilly band The Cultic Heads.

Nick Kemp.

For anyone who regularly attends Rockabilly/Psychobilly gigs you will no doubt have seen or been in the same venue as Nick Kemp. With a camera around his neck and a pair of glasses perched down his nose, Nick documents, photographs and reviews many shows. He currently writes The Psychobilly Corner for UK Rock 'N' Roll magazine and reviews gigs and records for them. Nick also wrote the definitive biography of Demented Are Go – Kicked Out of Hell, which took a lot of his skill and determination to weave their story into a cohesive narrative, he also managed to gain the trust of Sparky and many former members of the band making it a very enjoyable, shocking and essential read. "I had a peach of a subject in Demented" he states. Nick is also not shy into going to the bar and getting his round in which is always a good attribute. As the following interview shows Nick's passion for the scene is boundless and shows no signs of diminishing. The answers provided by Nick were via email:

The first rather obvious question is what is Nick's opinion why the Psychobilly/Rockabilly scene has been ignored by the music press for so many years?

Q. Psychobilly has never been cool. To the untrained ear it is 1950s music played badly. But to the cognoscenti there is a lot more going on, there is a huge amount of unappreciated musicianship. Take Dick Thomas (former Demented Are Go guitarist) for example he was an absolutely fabulous player, but I suppose the subject matter of Psychobilly always ensured that it would never be taken seriously by the rather earnest music press. I suppose the dancing – wrecking - which, to the untrained eye looks like violence probably also helped to scare the press away from the scene. But it has always been a very diverse scene and one can imagine that a band like Restless, might have been tolerable to a mainstream audience, the same was true of the Long Tall Texans and they certainly played a lot of support slots beyond the confines of the scene, I remember for example seeing them support The Cardiacs at the Marquee Club in the very early 1990s. I suppose that the fact that the biggest band on the scene The Meteors, has such a poor ambassador for the scene in the shape of Paul Fenech can't have helped matters. The scene has belatedly got some coverage in the music press in Vive le Rock magazine, but I put that down to the efforts of one man, Simon Nott, who is both very articulate and has been passionate about Psychobilly for many years. Oh, and the same is true of Craig Brackenridge who has taken Psychobilly to the pages of Vintage Rock.

Q. Why has Psychobilly never gone mainstream?

A. I suppose that King Kurt gained some mainstream attention in the mid-eighties, but it was only ever as a sort of novelty act, they got onto Top of the Pops. The Highliners, also got into the charts with Henry the Wasp, but again that was very much a novelty song. It was good for a laugh, but nothing more. With the exception of ABC and ID Records, both of which were short-lived there really weren't any record labels that would touch Psychobilly, except of course Roy Williams at Nervous Records who put out some classic albums by the likes of Batmobile and the Frantic Flintstones. But come the turn of the decade, the 1990s there was very little record label interest with Link Records' Chuck Flintstone Presents series and occasional releases from Dell Richardson's Fury Records providing the only outlet for bands on the scene. The Meteors were a bit different as the big band on the scene having the support of Anagram Records for a long time.

Q. Do you think Psychobilly can be classed as elitist and difficult to penetrate for those who wish to explore it?

A. I don't feel elitist in the slightest. I would much rather our scene pulled in a more diverse and larger audience. It would certainly benefit enormously from a younger audience. It is also a largely working-class phenomenon, I wish that it was more diverse, ethnically too.

Q. You have also played drums in a few bands the most well-known being The Coffin Nails.

A. I played drums from the age of fourteen. I wrote a letter some years later to Steve Clarke of the Coffin Nails' fame, when I joined their fan club, to the effect that if you're ever in need of a drummer let me know. Some years later in 1994 I think that it was he got in touch. We had two rehearsals, but that was it. I was doing a Master's degree at the LSE at the time and my drums had been in the loft for two or three years, so I really wasn't very good. Fast-forward twenty years, my wife had gone back to university to do a PGCE and I had recently discovered that there was a Psychobilly community online. I answered an on-line add for a drummer for a female fronted Psychobilly band. The band turned out to be the Screamin' Sugar Skulls with whom I have many fond memories. On one occasion we supported the Coffin Nails at the Blomsbury Bowling Lanes. I must have convinced the band that I could play because a little while later Scott go in touch to see if I could help the band out playing at Ginger Meadham's wedding. We had two rehearsals and then played the gig, but we weren't very good. Then there was a headline gig at the 12 Bar that went rather well. This was followed by a gig at Fibbers on Holloway Road for Peter Jagusch's fortieth birthday party which I didn't think went very well because I couldn't hear anything. I then had a phone call asking whether I could accompany the band to the US for the West Coast Rumble, I knew that the headmaster wouldn't grant me permission so regretfully I had to bow out. I then became a House Master at school, so I had to bow out of music. Unfortunately, I lasted only two terms before suffering a cardio-respiratory arrest which has left me with Parkinsonian features one of which is poor balance and almost no sense of rhythm. Sadly, I am unable to play the drums, I have filled the void by writing about music – which does help.

I am an historian by training, so it was the perfect thing for me to do, to twin my passion the music with my facility. Out of the blue, Simon Nott, whom I knew, invited me to write a review of the Bedlam Breakout festival that I had just attended. It took me about twenty minutes to write. I had actually penned some gig and album reviews on Facebook, that, I suspect Simon had seen and so he thought that I'd be a relatively safe pair of hands. Recently, Simon stepped down from his monthly Psychobilly Corner in UK Rock & Roll Magazine and again Simon invited me to take over, so I have done so".

Q. Strangely Nick is not a major record collector. I ask why.

A. I am not nearly as serious a collector as Richard Smith (another well-known face at many a gig). In fact, to be honest, and I know that this will sound sacrilegious to many, but my favourite format is CD.

Q. Although Nick admits to being too young to be a Klub Foot regular, he did attend the now legendary gig at the Town and Country Club after the Klub Foot closed featuring the GuanaBatz. Does Nick agree that the closure of the Klub Foot was a strong contributing factor for the scenes decline within the UK at the time?

A. Yes, absolutely. The closure of the Klub Foot robbed the scene of its one key meeting point. Despite efforts to regenerate the Klub Foot at the Boston Arms, and despite efforts to create a new centre at the LMS in Hendon, nothing ever worked. This, of course, coincided with the rise of Madchester and acid house. Whilst I was never able to make that transition it seems that many people who liked to get shitfaced and dance themselves silly at the Klub Foot were quite happy to switch from Snakebite to Es and a different form of dancing.

Q. Aren't a few of those older Psychobilly's now returning to the scene?

A. I think that it is really just being able to. A lot of the older generation who left the scene to settle down and have kids, have now a second wind as their kids have flown the nest. Facebook has been instrumental in helping people rediscover the scene.

Q. But is the scene attracting a younger audience which it needs to obtain for it to survive?

A. In this country the audience at Psychobilly gigs is an aged and aging one. On the continent there is far more new blood. I don't think that it's a matter of the older audience making the young folk feel unwelcome either. I went to Club Sin in Tampere Finland a few years ago to see the Demented Scum Cats play a festival and there I was struck both by the variety of bands on the bill, but even more so by the diversity of the punters. It seemed that all varieties of alternative types descended on the venue: Punks, Rockabillies, Psychobilly's, Skinheads, Metal Kids, Emos, the whole gamut. It's for a similar reason that I am not averse to cross-pollination of Psychobilly and Death Metal for example. I think here, for example of Finland's Graveyard Bashers, who whilst not really my cup of tea, help to bring Psychobilly to a new audience.

Q. What fires Nick's interest and continuing enthusiasm for the scene?

A. For me, it is all about the music – I just absolutely love it. I live and breathe Billy music. I don't really look Psychobilly, I don't have any tattoos and I don't have my ear-pierced (yet), I have met some lovely people on the scene who I count amongst my best friends, but for years I used to go to gigs on my own, speak to no -one, so it was not the social side that attracted me.

Q. Finally, the interview can't conclude without mention of Demented Are Go. I am interested in finding out what Nick regards as their best album.

A. To me Kicked Out of Hell is one of the greatest albums of all time. It certainly took Psychobilly to a whole other level. Every song is superb and the production in immaculate. It really is an absolute gem - the musicianship of Lex Luther, Graeme Grant, Ant Thomas and Mark Phillips was quite exceptional.

Nick Kemp can definitely be regarded as an important person on the scene. If it wasn't for people like Nick, the scene would have fewer supporters as he continues to share his knowledge and enthusiasm through social media and printed word. He often travels around the country (and even abroad) catching gigs and buying many of the new releases. The scene needs more like him for it to survive further into the twenty first century.

Restless.

September 2021 Restless were headlining at The Rubberneckin' Rockin' Club in Harrow, the venue disappointedly was far from packed, I spotted Mark Harman at the bar and after a little encouragement from my wife approached him and asked if he remembered the interview I conducted with him and the band at the Klub Foot during the eighties, with candour Mark responded that he did not, but far from being discouraged I decided to regale him with details about this obviously forgettable experience. I found Mark to be friendly and approachable and asked if he would be interested in being featured within this book, fortunately he agreed. The only downside to this is his insistence that he would answer my questions via email and not during a face-to-face interview. I later contacted Ben Cooper the bands drummer who also agreed but again wanted the answers via email. Jeff Bayly who at the time was the bass player also agreed to answering via email. So, after frantically cobbling sets of questions together I emailed them to each member. Both Mark and Jeff kindly sent their answers back, Jeff in fact in a remarkably fast time, but Ben after receiving them decided to refrain, "really sorry, don't think I'm going to be able to do this" he curiously messaged me.

The following are Marks answers.

Q. When you were recording Why Don't You Just Rock did you have any idea at the time that it was something special and would still be regarded as influential many years later?

A. We knew it was going to be different that's for sure. When I say different, I mean the band were not just going to be another covers trio re-hashing Vincent and Presley authentic stylie. We had an agenda and that was to bring rockin' music into a modern world. After putting down 'Scam' and 'Ice cold' it became pretty evident that something was happening to Rockabilly music. It was a very exciting time for us and all involved in the making of 'Why Don't you just Rock'

Q. Was the recording of the follow up Do You Feel Restless not as smooth?

A. No, anticlimactic I'd say. After the fun and energy, we'd effortlessly put into our first album we found the formula had changed in that we recorded in an unfamiliar studio with equipment we didn't like (electronic drums???!!). It seemed a world apart from our first album and Octopus studios. I still say Ben's great songs saved the day, but we didn't particularly enjoy recording Do you feel.

Q. Your contribution to the Stomping at The Klub Foot album introduced Restless to a larger audience, leading to Restless becoming one of the top headlining bands there. What are your views and memories of that legendary venue.

A. Klub Foot was the bridge to modern rockin' music, without it I wonder if we would have become so popular. People were bored of the tried and tested cover/authentic scene and wanted something new and exciting......the Klub Foot showcased many modern rockin' bands who had the same idea as the young fans.

Q. After Midnight was like Marmite, meaning some people liked it and some didn't like the more polished commercial sound. I think it has stood the test of time well. Your opinion?

A. I sat on the fence for a long time over this album. With all good intentions, our management and record company wanted to take the whole thing to another level ....they threw copious amounts of money at the project and almost reinvented us! The album has stood the test of time and is now among the favourites for fans. It took a long time for it to be accepted.......it wasn't really us even though we wrote all the songs. Session men and production values took precedent over the core Restless sound. It was great fun making the record though! I have come to love it for many reasons memories being one of them.

Q. Do you ever regret ABC Records pushing the band in that

direction, i.e. glossy photos, poster with the album. Did it help or hinder the bands career?

A. See above really. It did alienate some hardcore Restless fans but at the same time, it opened up other doors for us......especially on the college and university circuit where we attracted a whole new raft of followers. I did regret it, but I don't anymore.

Q. In my original interview with you, you stated that: 'it's a bit of a bind' being classed as a Rockabilly band, due to the music not being classed in Ben's term as: 'trendy'. Do you still feel that?

A. No, not a bind. At the time we wanted to be big and famous. The scene has given Restless a 40+year longevity......cannot argue with that. Nowadays, we're proud to be classed as a Rockabilly band even more proud to be acknowledged as a pioneering neo-Rockabilly band!

Q. Would you describe yourself as a perfectionist? As the bands live performances and recordings are always of a high standard.

A. Well we don't rehearse, and I don't practice......we just play what we love and what we're good at. No science involved....just good Rock 'n' Roll!

Q. Did it get frustrating in the early days by getting associated with the Psychobilly scene?

A. No....it was good for us. In fact, I still don't know any other rockin' bands who are accepted at Rockabilly, Psychobilly, Country, Blues and Rock festivals. We play them all Psychobilly did nothing but help us.

Q. How big an influence is Elvis?

A. For me, Elvis is everything. I would never have gone anywhere near music if it hadn't been for him. I can't speak for the others but yes, a colossal influence.

Q. Why did you move to The Madhouse Recording Company for your next studio album Beat My Drum? What are your opinions on that album now?

A. I love Beat My Drum.......we had a lot of freedom making that ....and limitless studio time. Pete Gage was an incredibly talented teacher, engineer and producer and it was at these sessions (some 24 hours straight) that I learnt so much from him.......and what a workhorse he was!! We simply went from ABC to Madhouse because it was a better proposition......and control was handed back!

Q. How big a contribution did Pete Gage play in the Restless story?

A. Because Pete had great connections in the music industry it was a no brainer to take up his offer as management. Pete did everything for us for many years securing hundreds of dates, being our live sound engineer, studio engineer/producer......did I mention driver? He got us the Radio One session on Saturday live at Maida Vale in London, supports for Clash, Ramones....the list is endless. Pete's contribution was massive.

Q. Did the band split up after Beat My Drum?

A. I don't remember. Restless have often 'split up' only to regroup again later due to popular demand ....this has happened many times!

Q. What is your opinion about the stripped down Kickin' into Midnight album.

A. I liked the idea of it even if I think it sounds a little weak compared to the original. The idea was to strip all of the session musicians off to reveal just the band as we originally intended. Pete Gage produced both versions.......I wonder if the stripped-down version should have been done with new ears......both Pete's and ours were pretty tired on this project by this time. Hundreds and hundreds of hours had gone into the production, and I think maybe we'd become a little sound blind to it!

Q. In my original interview with you, I asked about the lack of coverage by the music press, how much better is it now for the band with the advent of social media?

A. I can't stand Facebook for a million reasons......but it has been great for the band. We can reach out, communicate, publicise, update and spread the news to our fans immediately. In that respect it is much better on a semi-personal basis. We do every now and again, get invited to do press/mag interviews which are always fun, but it is what it is.

Q. What is your opinion on streaming sites like Spotify?

A. Our music royalties have been killed by streaming services. I'll never know how they got away with it. Our only source of revenue nowadays is by playing live and to a lesser extent, selling merch.

Q. You've had other projects such as The Space Cadets and Loosenoose any other plans outside of Restless?

A. Not right now......it's time to celebrate the 40th Anniversary of Why Don't You Just Rock.......and with another Restless album in the pipeline we'll be busy enough. I do, however, have a contract for a solo album but as yet, no dates to start recording.

Q. How did Steve Whitehouse come to join the band?

A. Jeff decided to leave the band in 1989 just as Pete Gage, our manager had secured us first time dates in Japan. Both Ben and I decided we'd go out with a bang......but only if we could guarantee the services of Steve......who was the one we thought (quite rightly as it turned out) was the only guy who ticked all the boxes for what was required! It's because of him, and the success of the Japanese gigs that we decided to keep going with this new line-up......and Restless survived yet another crisis!!

Q. Figure It Out is one of my personal favourite albums of any genre, how did it come about and what are your feelings about it now?

A. One of my faves to. We had a great time making this and total freedom to choose songs and to produce it. Our old record company Nervous offered us a good budget and full control over the whole thing as a one-off. We got to work with a wonderful engineer called Sean Kirkpatrick who died far too young. I always think of him when I hear any track from this record. I'm very proud of it.

Q. Did Led Zeppelin legend Robert Plant perform on stage with the band?

A. We played at Robert Plants son's wedding, and he did indeed join us on stage. He was fantastic and knew all the songs we played (at his request), things like Such a Night and Say Mama to name a few. He basically sang the whole second set. What a great night, what an even greater guy.

Q. What made the Klub Foot line up reform?

A. It was a logical step for the band after Paul left. People were always asking if it could be possible. Those Klub Foot years were very successful for us and so I asked both Jeff and Mick if they'd like to put in a year one more time as the four piece and they said yes....and away we went. It was great to work with them again.

Q. What are the plans for Restless in the future? Will the original Klub Foot line up continue?

A. Sadly, as we speak (Jan 2022) the Klub Foot line-up has once again come to an end. Jeff has left to pursue other interests and as it is the 40th Anniversary of our very first album, we're going to revert back, once again, to the original three-piece line up of me, Ben and Paul to celebrate this milestone. What I can tell you is that all of the musicians who have appeared in whatever line-up over the years are still great friends so anything can happen at anytime.....but even now, there seems to be no end to what has, so far, been an incredible rockin' journey!

Here are Jeff's answers, who at the time was Restless' bass player.

Q. How daunting was it to join Restless after Paul Harman left.

A. I wasn't an outsider joining the band with the attitude that I had to impress the guys. I was close friends with Mark, Ben and Paul even before Restless played their first gig. I had faith in my ability and obviously Mark and Ben did to. So, it was more excitement than anything else that I had the opportunity to join the band.

Q. Had you been in any bands previously?

A. My first band experience was a band called Wild Asylum... actually with Mick Malone. We only played a handful of gigs. Just a point of interest though our first gig was at Springlands Social Club where Restless played their first gig. My next band was a little bit more prolific with work. The band was called the Del – Rays hailing from Exeter in Devon. It's crazy looking back now but I used to get the National Express coach from Suffolk to Devon every weekend to play in the band. I eventually moved to Exeter for a little while before moving back to Sudbury to join Restless.

Q. The bands contribution to the Stomping at The Klub Foot album introduced Restless to a larger audience, leading to Restless becoming one of the top headlining bands there. What are your views and memories of that legendary venue?

A. After 40 years of playing in various bands even now if people ask about the best gigs, I've been involved with it's the Klub Foot days hands down. We were all young, things were happening and the gigs themselves were just so wild and exciting. If we had a gig at the Klub Foot that day I would have a buzz from the moment I woke up. Great times.

Q. After Midnight was like Marmite, meaning some people liked it and some didn't like the more polished commercial sound. I think it has stood the test of time well. Your opinion?

A.I have a unique perspective about the After Midnight album. It was the first studio album that I was involved with so it will always be special to me. It's strange I do love it but at the same time there are issues with the production for me. I can see how it must have come as a shock to some... definitely a departure from the Restless format. It's a product of its time though and personally I have no regrets at all about trying to push the band to a wider audience.

Q. In my original interview with the band, Mark stated that: 'it's a bit of a bind' being classed as a Rockabilly band, due to the music not being classed in Ben's term as: 'trendy'. Do you feel that? Did the Rockabilly tag hold the band back a bit?

A. I'm not sure the Rockabilly tag was a hindrance to the band, after all the early to mid-eighties was the heyday for Rockabilly...so many of our contemporaries made it to the charts. To this day I'm still a little surprised that Restless couldn't emulate that success when it came to the national charts... maybe our departure from the straightforward Rockabilly format was the reason...who knows?

Q. Would you describe the band as perfectionists? As the bands live performances and recordings are always of a high standard

A. Being a perfectionist and achieving perfection are two different things. Yes the band are perfectionists...but, personally I haven't recorded one single track that in my opinion is perfect. I think I can speak for the other guys on that one to. When you are in the studio and you have four members of a band, say a couple of engineers, they will all have a different opinion. You produce the best product possible. but it's objective, it will never be perfect.

Q. Was it a help or hinderance being so closely associated with the Psychobilly scene in the early days?

A. I'm not actually sure on this one...we can all look back in hindsight, but it was what it was. Of course we played the likes of the Klub Foot etc but we were also very busy on the college and university circuit ...this was probably the bulk of our work at that time ..so I guess we had the best of both worlds

Q. Who are your influences?

A. In the late seventies we had a local band in our home town of Sudbury called Rockhouse . They were well respected on the scene, and I used to tag along to the gigs, help carry the equipment etc. Became good friends with the bass player Bob Plumb. Incidentally Rockhouse are still playing today and I'm still great friends with Bob. Anyway...at the gigs I thought Bob looked so cool. I wanted to be up there on stage playing the bass. Bob was a bit of a hero to me, and I would say was my biggest inspiration and influence.

Q. What is your opinion about the stripped down Kickin' into Midnight album?

A. I thought the idea of giving the After Midnight album the RESTLESS treatment was a sound idea, however... whenever I listen to it, it leaves me cold, just my personal opinion but I think the production is not what it could or should have been.

Q. Did the band split up after Beat My Drum? and why did you leave?

A. There were a couple of reasons why I left the band. It's beyond question that the mid to late eighties were the busiest time in the band's long history. We were doing up to 28 shows a month and that did actually take its toll on my health. I was starting to have seizures that apparently were put down to stress. Not only that but about this time I had a new partner who had two young children. It was a case of needing a steady reliable income. Trucking was in my family and my blood, so this was the obvious time to put myself through the HGV license and move on with my life.

Q. You joined Mark in Loosenoose what other projects were you involved in?

A. Loosenoose was a great project started from scratch...short lived but produced one of my favourite albums. Which incidentally Mark and myself produced and recorded in my spare bedroom over a three-month period. I've played in a few well-established bands on the scene over the years ...but not a whole heap regarding projects.

Q. What made the Klub Foot line up reform?

A. Personally I've always harboured hopes that maybe the four piece could get back together to do just a couple of shows at some point just for pure nostalgia's sake. We had mentioned it in passing over the years, but nothing ever came of it. When Paul announced he was retiring from the band about 4 years ago it just seemed the natural progression. I have been working with Mark on and off over the years in one way or another even depping on the odd Restless show, so was just a matter of getting Mick back on board.

Q. Were you surprised at the very positive reaction about the line up playing again?

A. I wasn't really surprised at the positive reaction...as I said before, the four-piece line-up was the busiest in the band's history...we made a lot of friends during this period. People have fond memories of their youth and we were a part of that.

Q. Covid appeared soon after the line-up reformed which must have had a huge impact involving cancelled tours etc, I noticed Paul Harman has played some gigs abroad.

A. Yes. This Covid business has definitely put a spoke in the wheels...not only Restless but all bands. I make no secret that I personally will not be having any injections...I have my views on this but that's for another time. We all know the situation regarding travel...it's nigh on impossible for me, I haven't even seen my girlfriend in almost two years as she's Portuguese and lives in Lisbon. So yes... that's the reason Paul is covering the foreign gigs for the time being.

Q. On a trivial night during my original interview with you, you stated that 'Trouble Rides a Fast Horse' was your favourite song off After Midnight, is that still the same?

A. At least I'm consistent...TRAFH is still my favourite off the album... although The Face is a close second.

Q. What are the plans for Restless in the future?

A. As most know Restless had planned on calling it a day ...but... the last two years have proved you can't take anything for granted and life is too short, so for the time being we are taking it a day at a time ...as it stands its full steam ahead and see what develops.

Unfortunately for Jeff as stated earlier he parted ways with the band, being replaced with original bass player and Marks brother Paul Harman. The band remain one of the top bands on the rockin' scene and are still able pack out the 100 Club for their first albums fortieth anniversary tour.

Dave Diamond.

Drummer in various bands, gig promotor, vintage drum collector, record collector and record reviewer. Dave Diamond is all of these but essentially, he is a fan of rockin' music be it Psychobilly, Rockabilly, Rock 'n' Roll or Garage/Trash, Dave is passionate about it all. He is a Rock 'n' Roll dynamo. If you start to talk about music, he will mention the most obscure artist or record and look bemused if you don't know who it is. His enthusiasm and excitement knows no bounds. Whereas some people might get enthused about a new car or a wide screen tv, Dave is over the moon to have purchased the acetate of The Bananamen's Love Me/Surfin' Bird a one off one sided cut of the classic single cut in Trident Studios in 1983 and used by the band to promote the release in record shops, Dave also got it signed by Bal, for Dave it doesn't get better than that.

The following interview was conducted within the garden of The Anchor Pub in Wingham in Kent, Dave's band Thee Escapees were due to play there that evening at a gig organised by Peter Hanscomb who also shares Dave's enthusiasm by putting on many bands within the pub such as The Masonics, The Hillmans and The Go Go Cult. The weather got a bit fresh for May, but Dave braved it with just a t shirt.

The first rather obvious question was how did Dave first get into rockin' music? "I was twelve my older brother is four years older than me and in 1978 he used to blast Gene Vincent and Johnny Burnette out of his bedroom. Even if I didn't like Rock 'n'' Roll I had no choice, it would just be blasting non-stop. I just got hooked. He was a biker going out on his Triumph and when he went out, I used to go into his bedroom and play all his records". Bands like Showaddywaddy and Darts were in the charts then, did they influence you? "My brother was die hard you didn't listen to music like that, guys in yellow and pink drapes. The only one I liked was Duke of Earl by Darts until I realised it was a cover version, that's plastic not proper Rock 'n' Roll. For me it was all Johnny Burnette,

Gene Vincent and Eddie Cochran". This was all to change in 1981: "One of the guys in my school Peter Clark had a quiff all shaved round the side and the back and at the bottom on the back of his head he had a little pigs tail dyed pink, he said to me you should come to Feltham Football Club there's a new band called The Meteors, I've bought their new record". Now curious, Dave went to Peter's house after school: "I think it was Radioactive Kid that he played and I was like what is this, it's amazing". Unfortunately, even though Dave was now infected with the Psychobilly disease he didn't go to the gig: "I was about five foot four, I thought there's no way I'm ever going to get in there, so we waited until we were eighteen. The first time we went there was 1984 and on the bill was The Meteors and 16 Guns and the venue had tables around the side and I remember standing on a table and everyone was wrecking, I thought this was amazing". For the next five years: "I was just full on, Johnny Burnette and Gene Vincent had gone although I still loved them, but I was more into the heavier Graveyards, Zombies, Earwigs in my Brain". The Meteors debut album In Heaven: "Was a game changer in my life and The Ricochets album Made in the Shade also had a massive effect on me".

It is inevitable that the Klub Foot would soon appear within Dave's horizon: "What memories there. The first time I went to the Clarendon was downstairs on the 03/02/1984, I saw The Vibes and The Surfadelics it cost me £1.50 to get in and I'm pretty sure Snakebite back then was 99p. The Vibes were probably the best garage band in my eyes ever. My first Klub Foot upstairs in The Clarendon was on 16/06/1984. I saw Guanabatz, Sting-Rays and Thee Milkshakes. I was then regularly attending the Klub Foot all the time and also going downstairs seeing all the great bands. What was great about it you had a mixture of bands like Mod with The Prisoners, Garage with The Vibes and Thee Milkshakes, neo Rockabilly with Restless and then you had what was termed Psychobilly with The Meteors, GuanaBatz and Demented Are Go. What an amazing time the Klub Foot was with all those different genres of bands on one night. You had your people with blond quiffs, you had Mods, you had Beatnik style and you had people from college who just loved music. There was never, ever any trouble apart from the wrecking where you might get a whack in the face but that was all part of it". Dave continues to reminisce: "In the early days I used to get a night bus home which was quite funny as I had a big blond quiff and you used to get all the smoothies at the back shouting 'Oi Elvis' you were running the gauntlet. Never any trouble but loads of verbal".

Dave decided it was time to form his own band The Bloodstains: "I was at Richmond College in 1984, I was a year older than Mike, Chris and Darren who were also in the band and were still at school. Mike used to live opposite my house, and we used to listen to the early Meteors together and he was also a really good writer of songs, and I also wrote songs". The band started to emerge when Mike: "Used to play the drums and I used to scream and make some noise singing. Mark could play guitar and Darren could roughly play the double bass". So, The Bloodstains were formed with: "Me singing, Darren on the bass, Mark on guitar and Mike on drums. Next up we had to think of a band name so me and Mike came up with The Bloodstains something gory to go with the graveyards and horror. We used to rehearse at Richmond College and all our friends used to come and watch us rehearse, we had about thirty to forty people, it was really mad". I briefly enter The Bloodstains story around this point, as I was communicating with Chris P who produced the 54321 fanzine. "We sent a demo off to Chris P whom I sort of knew from the Clarendon and we used to buy the 54321 fanzine. I remember saying to him that we were in a band called The Bloodstains and he wanted to hear us, so me and Mike taped ourselves at Richmond College which we sent off to Chris P". Chris P soon featured the band in his fanzine 54321 giving the band a page with my dodgy Psychobilly drawing on it, Dave jokes: "I dunno who did the drawing". A gig with the GuanaBatz was also offered: "Chris P said do you fancy having a gig with the GuanaBatz but we were nowhere near playing a gig". So, the band turned it down and fell apart, as Dave explains: "The Bloodstains were building up, but Mike went to college and ended up at the airport, Mark went to college and dropped out after six months and not sure what happened to Darren, basically no one was at college it was just me. Mark went off the scene, Darren was still on the scene and Mike was on the scene. We were too busy watching bands to do our own, (sighs) what might have been".

A while later Dave stopped going to the Klub Foot: "The reason we stopped going was because the bands were getting a lot more faster and the sound I loved from those early days was disappearing, I stopped going about a year before it closed as the new bands coming through I thought weren't good, it was late '87 by then". Dave started reconnecting to his Rockabilly roots: "The Hemsby weekenders were starting which took me all the way back to Johnny Burnette and Gene Vincent again. The rockin' scene in the late eighties and nineties was thriving, weekenders and gigs with Joe Clay coming over from America and The Comets came over". For Dave: "Psychobilly took a back seat, Rock 'n' Roll is in my heart and my soul, and they do say once you have the bug it will be with you forever". Dave even started playing in bands again: "It was ten years after The Bloodstains in 1994 I was in a band called The Untamed, we did a single called Wiggle Shakin' Mama which sold five hundred copies which was quite fast neo-Rockabilly". Other bands include The Sundowners, The Hi-Fi's and Thee Escapees to name a few. Dave also created his own record label Diamond Discs.

The Boomerang Club in London is a club Dave organises and runs. Dave explains how it started: "I'd always said to my wife Susie why aren't certain bands booked to play in London, if I ran a club I'd book those bands and put them on, whether it was a band from Devon or a band from Scotland and not always the same London bands playing London as the London scene is quite cliquey sometimes. Susie said why don't you run your own club. My really good friend Andy Edwards said that he would go in half with me if I ran the club and booked the bands, he'd be the money guy as he's really good with spreadsheets. So, I'm the face of The Boomerang Club but without Andy there would be no club. We have a mixture of Beat, Rock 'n' Roll, neo-Rockabilly and Garage bands all playing the same event at the club. People have actually come up to me and said that it's like the Klub Foot because it's all different genres". At the time of writing five nights had sold out.

Finally, Dave explains why he is still so enthusiastic about the rockin' scene: "I just love my music, love my Rock 'n' Roll and all genres of it, I just love it all from Gene Vincent to The Meteors, Little Richard to the GuanaBatz and now I'm playing music and sometimes sharing a stage with my idols, I still feel like I'm on cloud nine. Ringing up bands I love and asking them to play The

Boomerang club, it's amazing". Final comment? "Let the good times roll".

Dave is proof that although the scene is over forty years old a person infected by the Psycho disease and the rockin' bug can still maintain the initial excitement and enthusiasm they felt all those years ago and in Dave's case even build on it. He even managed to make the cover of the UK Rock 'n' Roll Magazine which he is immensely proud of. So, if you're not buying his records or attending one of his gigs you probably will within the future as he shows no sign of letting up.

About The Author

In Paul's teenage years during the 1980's he was totally captured by the Psychobilly, Garage and Rockabilly scene. He couldn't play an instrument and really didn't have the patience to learn but really wanted to get recognised within the scene. He had an inquisitive mind and decided to attempt to produce a fanzine which would give him the opportunity to meet and question many of the bands whose records he was so religiously buying.

The first interview he conducted was with arguably the biggest Psychobilly band in England - The Meteors. This set-in motion a series of interviews with other bands and musicians within the scene, many of whom had not been given any exposure from the English music press.
Many a Saturday afternoon saw him spending his hard-earned cash to jump on the train and travel up to the legendary Psychobilly venue in Hammersmith, The Klub Foot, a few interviews were actually conducted there.

His fanzine was called 'The Crazed' and lasted for just four issues, but featured interviews with quite a few of the leading 80's Psychobilly/Rockabilly bands, such as The Meteors, GuanaBatz, Demented Are Go, Restless and more.

For a while within the 1980's the scene shone, but like most things, eventually faded along with his enthusiasm for producing the fanzine.

'The Crazed' became a yellowing photocopied memory put away in a drawer and forgotten about for years.

It wasn't until many years later that 'The Crazed' emerged again in Craig Brackenridge's book about Psychobilly, 'Hell Bent on Rockin'. Parts of Paul's interview with the GuanaBatz was also featured within the CD booklet for Cherry Red Records re-release of their second album, 'Loan Sharks'. Paul was then interviewed about 'The Crazed' by the 'Ole School Psychobilly' website and this led to the genesis of the idea for the book.

The creation of 'The Crazed' book has been quite a journey, with new friendships made, and a few lost.

Old friendships were resurrected, with an understanding of why some of those were never maintained.

Paul travelled back to those heady times in the 80's where music and fashion ruled his life and re-captured his enthusiasm for the Psychobilly / Rockabilly scene.

Paul lives in Kent with his family and still maintains a strong interest in many different genres of music.